Shaping the Local Economy
Current Perspectives on Economic Development

Edited by
Cheryl A. Farr

**International
City
Management
Association**

PRACTICAL MANAGEMENT SERIES
Barbara H. Moore, Editor

Shaping the Local Economy
Capital Financing Strategies for Local Governments
Creative Personnel Practices
The Entrepreneur in Local Government
Human Services on a Limited Budget
Microcomputers in Local Government
Telecommunications for Local Government

The Practical Management Series is devoted to the
presentation of information and ideas from diverse
sources. The views expressed in this book are those of
the contributors and are not necessarily those of the
International City Management Association.

Library of Congress Cataloging in Publication Data
Main entry under title:
Shaping the local economy.
  (Practical management series)
  Bibliography: p.
  1. Industrial promotion—United States—Addresses,
essays, lectures.   2. Industry and state—United States—
Addresses, essays, lectures.   3. Local government—United
States—Addresses, essays, lectures.   I. Farr, Cheryl A.,
1955-   . II. Series.
HC110.I53S53   1984   338.973   84-6693
ISBN 0-87326-034-1

Printed in the United States of America.
12345 • 90898887868584

Foreword

The long-term health and vitality of a community depend in large part on the creation and implementation of a sound and intelligent economic development strategy. Local officials can—indeed must—take an active role if the community's future is not to be left to the decisions of others.

As its title implies, *Shaping the Local Economy* shows how local officials can do just that—how they can form working relationships with private-sector actors and use tax incentives, public capital, regulatory reform, and other tools to influence development decisions to the mutual benefit of public and private participants. The book also suggests ways to organize an effective program; outlines such common strategies as encouraging high-technology development, retaining existing businesses, and revitalizing commercial districts; and describes successful local programs.

This book is part of the continuing Practical Management Series, which is devoted to serving local officials' needs for timely information on current issues and problems.

We are grateful to the organizations that granted ICMA permission to reprint their material and to Cheryl A. Farr of the ICMA staff, who organized and compiled the volume. Thanks also go to David S. Arnold, who was of great help in planning the entire Practical Management Series.

William H. Hansell, Jr.
Executive Director
International City
    Management Association

Shaping the Local Economy:
Current Perspectives on Economic Development

The International City Management Association is the professional and educational organization for chief appointed management executives in local government. The purposes of ICMA are to strengthen the quality of local government through professional management and to develop and disseminate new approaches to management through training programs, information services, and publications.

Managers, carrying a wide range of titles, serve cities, towns, counties, and councils of governments in all parts of the United States and Canada. These managers serve at the direction of elected councils and governing boards. ICMA serves these managers and local governments through many programs that aim at improving the manager's professional competence and strengthening the quality of all local governments.

The International City Management Association was founded in 1914; adopted its City Management Code of Ethics in 1924; and established its Institute for Training in Municipal Administration in 1934. The Institute, in turn, provided the basis for the Municipal Management Series, generally termed the "ICMA Green Books."

ICMA's interests and activities include public management education; standards of ethics for members; the *Municipal Year Book* and other data services; urban research; and newsletters, a monthly magazine, *Public Management*, and other publications. ICMA's efforts for the improvement of local government management—as represented by this book—are offered for all local governments and educational institutions.

About the Editor and Authors

Cheryl A. Farr is an Assistant Director of ICMA's Office of Information Services. She has staffed a variety of economic and community development programs administered by ICMA, including EDA-sponsored projects on creating economic development strategies for small and medium-sized communities and HUD-sponsored projects on reducing housing costs through regulatory reform and using corporate strategic planning techniques in the public sector. Previously, she worked in the Economic Development Department of Danvers, Massachusetts. She received a master's degree in city and regional planning from Harvard University in Cambridge, Massachusetts, and a B.A. degree from Rutgers University in New Brunswick, New Jersey.

Following are the affiliations of the other contributors to *Shaping the Local Economy* at the time of writing:

Patricia Adell, Director of Program Development, Philadelphia Industrial Development Corporation.

Robert M. Ady, Senior Vice President, Fantus Company (an industrial location consulting firm).

James J. Bellus, Head, Department of Planning and Economic Development, St. Paul, Minnesota.

Edward deLuca, Director, Department of City Development, Pittsburgh, Pennsylvania.

Michael A. Dobbins, Architect, Department of Community Development, Birmingham, Alabama.

Kenneth P. Fain, Managing Editor, *Lenders Community Investment Report*, Washington, D.C.

Stephen B. Friedman, Deputy Director of Real Estate Consulting, Laventhol & Horwath, Chicago, Illinois.

Lawrence Hall, Neighborhood Assistance Coordinator, Office of Housing and Neighborhood Development, New Haven, Connecticut.

Ruth Knack, Managing Editor, *Planning* magazine, American Planning Association, Chicago, Illinois.

Karen LaFrance, Senior Planner, Pittsburgh, Pennsylvania.

Larry Ledebur, Senior Research Associate in Urban Economic Development, The Urban Institute, Washington, D.C.

Robert H. Lurcott, Planning Director, Pittsburgh, Pennsylvania.

Bruce W. McClendon, Director of Planning, Beaumont, Texas.

John Naisbitt, President, the Naisbitt Group, Washington, D.C.

Lawrence D. Rose, City Manager, Mercer Island, Washington.

Albert Shapero, William H. Davis Professor of American Free Enterprise Systems, Ohio State University, Columbus, Ohio.

Richard Starr, Vice President, Real Estate Research Corporation, Chicago, Illinois.

Glen Weisbrod, Senior Associate and Manager for Urban Analysis, Cambridge Systematics, Inc., Cambridge, Massachusetts.

Harold Wolman, Senior Research Associate in Public Finance, The Urban Institute, Washington, D.C.

Contents

Introduction   1
Cheryl A. Farr

PART 1
Change: The Local Economy and the Local Government Role

From an Industrial Society to an Information Society   9
John Naisbitt
Entrepreneurship in Economic Development   12
Albert Shapero
Concepts of Public–Private Cooperation   25
Harold Wolman and Larry Ledebur

PART 2
Organizing for Economic Development

Community/Economic Development: Local
Responsibilities   35
Richard Starr
Setting Up Shop for Economic Development   41
Ruth Knack, James J. Bellus, Patricia Adell
Organizing and Operating a Development Department   50
Edward deLuca

PART 3
Public Sector Intervention in the Marketplace

Leveraging: The Patchwork Quilt Approach to
Development   61
Kenneth P. Fain
Assessing Public Incentives for Private Development   66
Stephen B. Friedman
Shifting Factors in Plant Location   79
Robert M. Ady
Can Ma and Pa Compete Downtown?   86
Glen Weisbrod
Revitalizing Downtown Retailing: Trends and
Opportunities   91
Urban Land Institute
Urban Infill: Its Potential As a Development Strategy   102
Real Estate Research Corporation
High-Technology Development: Local Initiatives   117
Office of Technology Assessment

No Lost Causes: Salvaging Neighborhood Shopping
Districts   135
    Lawrence Hall, Robert H. Lurcott, Karen LaFrance, Michael A.
    Dobbins
Reforming Zoning Regulations to Encourage Economic
Development   145
    Bruce W. McClendon
Bloomfield, Connecticut: Helping Plants Grow Better   153
    Cheryl A. Farr
Negotiating Business Development: The Manager As
Broker   162
    Cheryl A. Farr and Lawrence D. Rose
Keeping Investment Dollars Home   183

For Further Reference

Introduction

Cheryl A. Farr

Planning and implementing economic development strategies is complex and time-consuming work for local governments. It requires nurturing a solid working relationship with key private-sector actors, capitalizing on available resources, and anticipating local, national, and international economic trends so that the community can benefit from them. Economic development demands a long-term perspective—investing staff and other resources today so that the community's future economic health will be stronger than it would be if left to the private sector.

Inherent in the public-private dichotomy is the fact that what's good for the whole isn't necessarily profitable for the individual. As a result, the public sector must take an active role in shaping the local economy, because decisions made by individual profit-oriented actors will often make use of local resources in ways that can negatively affect the community in the long run. The profit seeker can move on to more fertile territory when the resources are depleted; the public sector cannot.

How can local officials create effective economic development strategies? This book is designed to stimulate thinking; it is far too brief to be a definitive text. The book provides an overview of issues that are central to developing an economic development strategy and offers practical advice on implementing some common strategies (such as encouraging high-technology development, retaining existing businesses, and revitalizing commercial districts). Case studies are provided to show some of these concepts in practice.

Part 1, focusing on changes in the local economy and the local government role, includes two articles that highlight national issues of particular interest to localities planning economic development programs. An excerpt from John Naisbitt's *Megatrends* describes a national shift from an industrial to an information society and what it means. Next, Albert Shapero discusses the key characteristics of entrepreneurs and suggests ways in which communities can nurture entrepreneurial activity—a useful strategy, since roughly 40 percent of all new jobs nationally are created by small businesses with less than 20 employees. Then Harold Wolman and Larry Ledebur review the most common forms of interaction between public- and private-sector institutions and focus on approaches that are designed to influence business decisions and behavior in noncoercive ways.

Part 2 introduces issues that local governments need to consider when organizing for an economic development function. Richard Starr recommends a careful assessment of past and current economic development strategies and their successes as a starting point in organizing future efforts. Ruth Knack, James J. Bellus, and Patricia Adell provide perspectives on one central organizational issue: whether the economic development function should be located within city government or outside (as a separate corporation). They draw on the decisions made in St. Paul and Philadelphia to clarify the benefits of each alternative. Finally, Edward deLuca focuses on the need to have a game plan—an overall strategy—for local economic development efforts and the importance of incorporating overall activities directed toward that strategy into the organizational plan.

Part 3 reviews some of the major tools and program orientations used in local economic development programs. First, Kenneth P. Fain discusses the concept of leveraging private investment and financing with public capital so that the private investment, in turn, will help create employment opportunities, tax base expansion, and economic vitality. Next, Stephen B. Friedman offers advice on how communities can assess the usefulness of the tax breaks and other incentives requested by private development projects. He recommends evaluating the project's contribution to achieving the city's established development objectives, analyzing the market support for the project and its financial feasibility given market conditions, and reviewing the incentive options available to determine what will help the project most at the least cost to the local government.

Robert M. Ady then reviews the cost and noncost factors that are considered in a facility location evaluation and their relative importance. Glen Weisbrod reviews some common public-private approaches to supporting downtown areas and their effectiveness in expanding the downtown retail market. Excerpts from the Urban Land Institute's publication, *Revitalizing Downtown Retailing*, discuss the basic steps involved in creating a retail development strategy and the public sector's role in encouraging public-private participation in such efforts.

The Real Estate Research Corporation's executive summary of its report on urban infill provides an overview of how the infill market functions and recommends tools and techniques for encouraging infill development. Last, an excerpt from *Encouraging High-Technology Development*, a background paper by the Office of Technology Assessment of the U.S. Congress, discusses local strategies used to support high-technology development and factors affecting the success of these local programs.

Part 4 presents examples of successful local economic development efforts and offers practical tips based on the experiences of communities that have accomplished some typical economic development objectives. "No Lost Causes: Salvaging Neighborhood Shopping Districts" discusses an incentive program geared to leveraging private investment by merchants and property owners in New Haven, Connecticut; the use of market studies as a tool for planning neighborhood strategies in Pittsburgh, Pennsylvania; and the success of physical improvements in revitalizing a neighborhood commercial center in North Birmingham, Alabama.

Next, Bruce McClendon discusses experiences with integrating regulatory reform and local economic development objectives in Beaumont, Texas. The city worked to ensure that economical and innovative development practices were encouraged so that development costs could be reduced without sacrificing the quality of development. Two case studies developed by ICMA highlight effective strategies for business retention and expansion. "Helping Plants Grow Better" looks at the organization and implementation of an overall business retention program, drawing on the experiences of Bloomfield, Connecticut. "Negotiating Business Development: The Manager As Broker" reviews the efforts of Mercer Island, Washington, to retain a major employer and the creative techniques local officials used to achieve broader economic development objectives in the process. The final article shows how active interest by private-sector actors in funding local business ventures stimulated economic growth in Chippewa Falls, Wisconsin.

Planning and implementing economic development strategies require a heavy investment of local officials' time and energy. But successful programs provide a healthy, diversified economic base that can weather national and local economic shifts, create job opportunities for community residents, and contribute to the development and maintenance of the community's quality of life. Planning for economic development is a process that typically includes the following tasks:

1. Evaluating past performance. Plans for the future should build on past successes and take advantage of the lessons learned from past failures. Evaluating both the programmatic and organizational history of earlier public and/or pri-

vate economic development programs is an important first step in planning a new economic development strategy. It can provide both direction and useful data that can make the planning job easier and more effective.

2. Recognizing major trends. It is important to know how healthy the community's existing businesses are and to compare and contrast local economic strengths and weaknesses with the national economy and the economies of comparable communities. This will help local leaders set program and policy directions by suggesting where investments might make the most sense. This task should include tracking political and social shifts as well as economic and technological changes.

3. Identifying internal strengths and weaknesses. Economic development strategies should be designed to take advantage of the strengths of the local public and private participants, including the resources each individual and organization controls and those to which they have access through their personal and professional relationships. Communities should not limit themselves to programs that rely on readily available resources—developing new strengths and compensating for existing weaknesses in available talents and resources is important. But recognizing, for example, that available staff have strong skills in financial packaging may mean that developing a revolving loan fund to leverage private investment may be more effective than initiating an employee training program for businesses, if staff have no expertise in the latter.

4. Defining overall program goals and alternative strategies. Many goals and objectives can and should be considered in the development of an action plan, but a successful program has just a few key goals and a thorough plan designed to accomplish them. Communities need to make choices—whether to focus on revitalizing downtown at the expense of neighborhood commercial centers during the next two years, for example, or whether to invest more resources in the expansion of existing industries than in attracting firms that would help diversify the economy.

5. Creating an implementation plan. Implementation strategies need to tie specific resources to goals and clarify tasks that will be accomplished in terms of specific time frames and actors with major responsibilities. Being specific about time frames and responsibilities provides information necessary for monitoring the ongoing implementation efforts.

6. Reexamining issues and policies. A method for integrating feedback from ongoing efforts as well as new information needs to be developed so that the strategy's directions are

constantly refined to meet the needs of a changing environment. As implied earlier, local officials need to continually track major trends and adjust policies and programs accordingly.

A well-planned and well-executed economic development strategy can lead to a stronger local economy. Familiarity with program and organization options is an important first step for local officials in designing an economic development program. Also necessary are an understanding of local resources, constraints, and opportunities and the commitment of resources, if the community wants to choose its path rather than be directed solely by the decisions of individuals seeking to maximize their personal financial return on investment.

PART 1

Change: The Local Economy and the Local Government Role

From an Industrial Society to an Information Society

John Naisbitt

The five most important things to remember about the shift from an industrial to an information society are:

- The information society is an economic reality, not an intellectual abstraction.
- Innovations in communications and computer technology will accelerate the pace of change by collapsing the *information float*.
- New information technologies will at first be applied to old industrial tasks, then, gradually, give birth to new activities, processes, and products.
- In this literacy-intensive society, when we need basic reading and writing skills more than ever before, our education system is turning out an increasingly inferior product.
- The technology of the new information age is not absolute. It will succeed or fail according to the principle of high tech/high touch.

The information economy is real

If we are to speak of an information economy, we must be able to measure it in concrete terms. How much of the nation's wealth is actually produced in the information sector? How many of us earn a living in information jobs?

Without answers to these questions, most of us will probably choose to pledge continued allegiance to the economic reality we have experienced firsthand, the industrial era, where we produced "real" goods with "real" price tags. We will dismiss the information economy as ephemeral paperwork existing only as an adjunct to goods-producing sectors.

Reprinted with permission from *Megatrends: Ten New Directions Transforming Our Lives* (New York: Warner Books, 1982).

Documenting the information economy is difficult, to be sure. Pinpointing the economics of the creation, production, and distribution of information requires quantifying and codification of highly detailed minutiae.

Fortunately, these questions have been asked and extensively answered in a landmark study by information specialist Dr. Marc Porat. Under the sponsorship of the U.S. Department of Commerce, Porat painstakingly dissected the nation's economy and established criteria for labeling a job or part of a job and its income as part of the information sector or the goods-producing sector, or something other.

"Stating precisely who is an information worker and who is not is a risky proposition," writes Porat. However, his study documents his conclusions extensively enough to convince the information economy's skeptics.

Porat sorted through some 440 occupations in 201 industries, identified the information jobs, and compiled their contribution to the GNP. Questionable jobs were excluded so that the study's conclusions err on the conservative side.

Porat's study is incredibly detailed. He begins with the obvious sorting-out and tallying-up of the economic value of easily identifiable information jobs such as clerks, librarians, systems analysts, calling this first group the *Primary Information Sector*. According to Porat's calculations for the year 1967, 25.1 percent of the U.S. GNP was produced in the Primary Information Sector, that is, the part of the economy that produces, processes, and distributes information goods and services. Included here are computer manufacturing, telecommunications, printing, mass media, advertising, accounting, and education, as well as risk-management industries, including parts of the finance and insurance businesses.

But Porat's study goes on to deal with the more difficult questions that have overwhelmed other researchers. How does one categorize those individuals holding information jobs with manufacturers and other noninformation firms? To answer this question required "tearing firms apart in an accounting sense into information and non-information parts."

Porat creates a new information grouping called the *Secondary Information Sector*. It quantifies the economic contribution of information workers employed in noninformation firms.

These workers produce information goods and services for internal consumption within goods-producing and other companies. In effect their information products are sold on a fictitious account to the goods-producing side of the company. The Secondary Information Sector generated an additional 21.1 percent of the GNP.

Porat's study concludes, then, that the information economy accounted for some 46 percent of the GNP and more than 53 percent of income earned. This was in 1967.

Porat is unwilling to estimate how much the information economy has grown since, except to say it has increased, "by leaps and bounds."

Porat's study leaves little room for doubt. David Birch's more recent finding that only 5 percent of the almost 20 million new jobs created in the 1970s were in manufacturing (almost 90 percent were in information, knowledge, or service jobs) further substantiates the fact that we are now a nation of information workers. For example, while the total labor force grew only 18 percent between 1970 and 1978, the number of administrators and managers grew more than three times that rate—58 percent. Health administrators grew at an astounding 118 percent; public officials were up 76 percent; bankers, 83 percent; systems analysts, 84 percent. In contrast, engineers grew by less than 3 percent.

New York City, once a leading light of industrial America, has lost half the manufacturing jobs it had in 1947. The city lost 40,000 manufacturing jobs in the years between 1977 and 1980 alone. In contrast, New York is experiencing a boom in information jobs. The Regional Planning Association estimates that more than half of New York's gross city product is now generated by people who work in information. In recent years, legal services have replaced apparel as New York City's leading export.

Several states are attempting to replicate the industry-to-information shift that seems to have occurred naturally in New York City. The key strategy is to offer more incentives to high-tech information companies:

- California's Governor Jerry Brown wanted the state to offer direct subsidies to high-tech information companies.
- In 1980 North Carolina invested millions in a new microelectronics research center. General Electric Company promptly decided to build a new plant nearby.
- The Minnesota legislature is considering financing the expansion of the University of Minnesota's microelectronics facility in order to attract more high-tech information firms.
- Ohio has established a $5-million fund to make direct loans to high-technology companies.

The cities, states, and companies that plan for the new information age will be in a key position to reap its rewards. And those rewards will be ample.

Entrepreneurship in Economic Development

—————————————————— Albert Shapero

The translation of policy and theory into workable action programs is an art form that is little understood and seldom practiced successfully. Nowhere is the gap between theory and useful action more apparent than in the field of economic development. This article is one effort to help close the gap between generalized goal statements and useful operational programs. More specifically, it is concerned with discussing and suggesting research efforts focused on eliciting and developing one aspect of entrepreneurship—company formations—at the local level.

Some aspects of local economic development

Contrasting Manchester and Birmingham, England, in the mid-nineteenth century, Jane Jacobs, the architectural writer and critic, seeks for clues to long-term dynamism at the community level. She points out that Manchester was held up by the knowledgeable writers of the period as a paragon of efficiency, the model of the future.[1] At that time in history, Britain dominated the world in textiles, and Manchester was the heart of Britain's textile industry. Cotton-textile manufacturing was concentrated in a small area around Manchester. The city was near the great port of Liverpool. The coal, the necessary pure water, the humid climate were available to make Manchester a natural hub of textile manufacturing. Supplementary and supporting industries, such as cotton-textile machinery and dye

Reprinted with permission from *Expanding the Opportunity to Produce: Revitalizing the American Economy through New Enterprise Development*, edited by Robert Friedman and William Schweke (Washington, D.C.: Corporation for Enterprise Development, 1981).

manufacturing, clustered nearby.[2] At the same time, Birmingham was

... precisely the kind of city that seemed to have been outmoded by Manchester.... Birmingham ... had no specialty of the kind that made Manchester's economy so comprehensible.... But as it turned out Manchester was not the city of the future and Birmingham was.... Manchester had acquired the efficiency of a company town. Birmingham had retained something different: a high rate of innovation. Indeed, Birmingham and London are the only two cities in Britain today that retain a significant capacity to create new work from their existing work....[3]

Reading Jacobs' description of Manchester and Birmingham suggests two aspects of development worth noting: (1) Economic development does not happen "in general," but to specific people in specific places; and (2) the goals of economic development at the local level must go beyond "increased jobs and income."

People identify themselves with domicile, community, and region. They act as if attachment to place is important in their decisions and actions. Increasingly, scholars are coming to accept this idea that few individuals act as economic maximizers responding rationally and instantaneously to perfect information about the economy. Rather, the population is seen to be made up of "satisfiers" and "suboptimizers" who are willing to forgo many obvious kinds of economic benefits for the sake of enjoying other less "rational" benefits. Consequently, it is reasonable that we seek out economic development approaches and programs that are geared for application at the community level, and that are capable of drawing upon and reflecting local peculiarities and predilections.

Despite the widespread preoccupation with economic development, we do not have a commonly accepted definition of economic development or its goals. Regional economic development policy is expressed in terms of "more jobs and more income." In addition, some regional development programs include goals in terms of "balanced growth," "fiscal stability," "equity," or some increment to GNP or regional exports. Unfortunately, as must be inferred from Jane Jacobs' description, more jobs, income, GNP, and regional exports were not enough to sustain Manchester. Set in somewhat broader and more formal terms, the goal of economic development for the lesser developed countries includes the notion of a continuing process, but leaves the process unspecified, "... a state in which the people have the material opportunities for using their talents, of living a full and happy life and steadily improving their lot."[4]

One might argue for a clearer picture of the characteristics that denote an area that has reached the desired state, and argue that the goals of development are more usefully stated in terms of processes than in terms of output. The essential differences between Manchester and Birmingham over a century ago were not differences in jobs, GNP, or income, but differences in certain dynamic qualities, such as the capability for innovation and self-initiated responses to events.

What we really want for an area (or more precisely, for the people within the area) is to achieve a state denoted by *resilience*—the ability to respond to changes in the environment effectively; *creativity* and *innovativeness*—the ability and willingness to experiment and innovate; *initiative taking*—the ability, desire, and power to begin and carry through useful projects. Preceding and accompanying the dynamic characteristics of resilience, creativity and innovativeness, and initiative taking is *diversity*. Obviously, diversity offers an area some measure of invulnerability to the effects of many unforeseen events and decisions; with diversity there is always part of the local economy relatively unaffected by changes in a single industry or marketplace or by legal constraints on a given product. Less obvious, but perhaps as important, diversity provides a favorable environment for creativity and innovativeness. Where variety and diversity abound, there is a higher likelihood for achieving meaningful associations of items not previously associated, one definition of creativity.

Local economic development programs too often concentrate on the more easily measured goals of more jobs and more income. Typically, a city or regional development authority launches an intensive campaign to attract large industrial plants in order to generate the targeted jobs and income. In the effort to attract large plants, many kinds of concessions are offered to the concerns being wooed: tax breaks, free or cheap land, long-term and low-interest loans, buildings, utility development, highway construction, railroad spurs. The probabilities of attracting a plant are overlooked, and the full consequences of attracting a major plant are not really understood. One study made in the late 1950s found that in the United States at that time there were approximately 16,000 development organizations competing for 200 available corporation moves; the efforts cost well over $250 million.

If the effort to obtain a plant succeeds, there is a high probability that the incoming company will bring its managers and highly skilled workers from other areas, while the local area provides the low-cost, unskilled workers. A flow is set up in which the skilled professionally trained youth of the community leave for other cities while the unskilled youth of the community and the unskilled workers of other communities are attracted and retained. The result of an in-migrating company, attracted by cheap labor and low costs, can be to lower the net quality of the human resources of a community.

With a large in-migrant company comes an enlarged work force. The new work force sets up a demand for all of the services that the cities provide their citizens—for police, fire protection, education, waste disposal. The tax demand goes up, but the incoming company frequently has been given a tax concession and is freed from paying the taxes generated by its presence.

Finally, the incoming company makes the community vulnerable. The community adjusts to the dominant source of jobs and income in the community, becomes dependent on it. The vulnerability is made apparent when it is suddenly realized that decisions about the local plant are made by a distant, uninvolved management that can easily shift its plant to a lower-cost region. Of course, managements are not eager to disrupt communities, and many corporations deliberately refuse to locate in a community where their decisions will have large social or economic effects.

Considering the negative economic and social consequences of dependence on a single crop, a single industry or a single resource (be it a mineral deposit or cheap manpower), it is surprising to find the extent to which local development officials still expend so much effort on attracting a single major corporate division to employ their "cheap" labor. A recent example of how the apparent short-term advantages gained through importing many industrial plants to provide jobs and income for local workers had long-term negative effects for a region can be found in the Mexican-American border program. In ten years the program attracted some 450 American manufacturers through the bait of low-cost labor. Now that wages are improving (though still low by any standard), the companies are leaving for Central America, the Far East, and Ireland where wages are lower yet. In 1974-1975 there was a 30 percent decrease in employment in the area, and 25 to 40 percent of the in-migrant American plants have closed down, moved to other regions, or severely reduced their operations, leaving a very serious social and political problem in their wake.[5]

If not through jobs and income, how then might we frame our economic development goals so that we can achieve the requisite diversity and develop the desired resilience, creativity and innovativeness, and initiative-taking in an area? A fairly reasonable case can be made for a program to elicit and develop entrepreneurship in the form of company formations in an area. A program with targets set in terms of company formation rates has the potential for generating and embedding the desired characteristics in an area. By its very nature, entrepreneurship is concerned with the introduction of variety, innovations, and new ventures in a locale. Company formation is initiative-taking behavior, and entrepreneurial responses are the operational expression of resilience or response to the environment in change. Describing Birmingham in the 1850s, Jacobs writes, "It was always a peculiarity of Birmingham that small household trades existed which gave the inmates independence and often led—if the trade continued good—to competence or fortune."[6] Jacobs goes on to state that many of these endeavors failed and that they did not constitute a majority of the city's industry. Nevertheless, Birmingham's peculiarity led to the development of a diverse, responsive, resilient capacity that serves the city 125 years later.

Entrepreneurship

Entrepreneurs and entrepreneurship have occupied the interest of scholars of economic development since the early nineteenth century when,

J. B. Say . . . in the French (Cantillon) tradition, was the first to assign to the entrepreneur—per se and as distinct from the capitalist—a definite position in the schema of the economic process . . . the entrepreneur's function . . . to combine the factors of production into a producing organism . . . he is the pivot on which everything turns . . . [7]

Throughout this article the term "entrepreneur" is used in the restricted sense of the "company former" or "company founder." All managers are not by definition entrepreneurs. Nor are all inventors. The entrepreneur brings together resources to organize and manage a new company. He is not necessarily the individual who conceived the idea for the company, invented the product or service manufactured and sold, or provided the capital.

The company formation process

The key questions of this article concern the company-formation process and how it may be elicited and supported for the economic development of an area or community.

Each year some hundreds of thousands of new businesses are formed in the United States. Each of these company formations is the culmination of a process that is affected by place and time, by the social economic climate, by the nature of the sector of the economy and of the individuals forming the company. Though each formation is a unique event, examination of the data for a large number of company formations in different countries, regions, and economic sectors suggests that there is a fairly consistent general pattern for the company-formation process. To be sure, the general pattern is highly complex and multivariate; nevertheless, a pattern can be discerned that goes a long way toward explaining the majority of formations. The general pattern includes four major elements that combine in an overdetermined manner, in that no single factor by itself accounts for the formations studied and no fixed distribution of the four elements applies to all formations. All four elements must be present though they are partially substitutable for each other.

The four major elements that go into the company-formation process are the following: (1) *displacement* of the nascent entrepreneur(s)—a situational variable; (2) an apparent *disposition to act* on the part of the nascent entrepreneur(s)—an individual psychological propensity; (3) examples of models of behavior that impart *credibility* to the act of forming a company for the nascent entrepreneur(s)—a social psychological or culturally contributed variable; and (4) *availability of resources* to the nascent entrepreneur for starting a new company—an economic variable.

Displacement   Most company formations are associated with some kind of personal displacement, some dislodgement from a comfortable or otherwise acceptable state of being. The displacements that initiate the company-formation process can be both negative and positive, externally imposed or internally perceived, and it is often a combination of negative pushes and positive pulls that combine to precipitate the actions leading to the formation of a company.

Disposition to act   Many people are displaced, but a relatively small percentage of them react to displacement by undertaking to form a company or, for that matter, by taking any major initiative with regard to their own futures.

Company formation is an extraordinary form of initiative taking. Initiative taking and the propensity to act are related directly to whether or not the individual feels that it is possible for him to affect events, to affect the world around him. Individuals can be differentiated in terms of whether they perceive the control of their lives to be *external*, determined by forces outside of themselves such as luck, fate, or other powerful people, or *internal*, in their own hands. Internal people are apt to be relatively self-reliant and to want autonomy and independence, hallmarks of the entrepreneur.

Imparting credibility to the act   Not everyone who is displaced and has a propensity to act turns his mind to starting a new company.

The most potent variable found associated with the company-formation act is the credibility of the act to the nascent entrepreneur. The individual must be able to see himself starting and operating a company, must be able to perceive himself in the role, or else he cannot even begin to think about the act. From the data available, it can be inferred that the way credibility is achieved is primarily by means of credible examples; company formations by someone "like one's self" or by someone with whom one can identify, someone drawn from the nascent entrepreneur's family or other of his reference groups. The most prevalent and prominent credible example is provided by one's father or mother.

The availability of resources   Initiative taking, the disposition to act, and credible examples are necessary but not sufficient for the formation of a company. The final required ingredient is resources.

The company-forming entrepreneur must directly possess the labor, materials, equipment, and facilities required for the potential venture or must obtain them by use of his or other people's capital. In times of readily available venture capital, the number of company formations goes up. In hard times, despite the displacement caused by job loss, the lack of available capital keeps the company-formation rate from rising.

The company formation process and local economic development

Programs to elicit and support the company formation process in a locale offer potential for economic development not readily available through other approaches. The following possibilities result from adding a program to encourage company formations to the economic development repertoire of an area.

1. An area capability for fielding appropriate responses to events in the marketplace as they occur. An area can develop a capacity to start successful new companies and, as a result, be better prepared to deal positively with whatever happens in the unknown future.

2. An actuarial approach to events. A multiplicity of companies, as differentiated from one or two corporate divisions, provides an area with a multiplicity of independent decision-making units with each assessing the environment from a somewhat different vantage point. A variety of assessments provides a higher likelihood of coming up with appropriate responses than can be obtained through one or two assessments.

3. A greater tendency to innovate. Each new company is an invention or innovation in itself. An increase in the number of companies formed in an area is an increase in innovative behavior by itself, and, as will be shown later in this article, each new formation (and innovation) raises the probability of the next one occurring.

4. Valuable social learning at very little political and economic risk. The positive effects of successful and growing enterprise are obvious; however, the benefits that accrue to an area from a failed, new and small enterprise are completely overlooked. A failed enterprise may be a highly traumatic experience for the founders and those who have financial stakes in the enterprise, but it is seldom a net loss for the community in which it occurs. Each failed enterprise is a generator of social learning for all those who have been associated with the enterprise: founders, employees, suppliers, bankers, lawyers, accountants, and customers. Empirical studies of company formations have shown that many successful entrepreneurs have failed at least once before their current success. Henry

Ford failed in business twice before he finally succeeded.[8] "... Individuals who previously owned a business have a much lower failure rate than those who have never been in business...."[9] If a community retains those who were a part of a failed enterprise, there may be little loss from the viewpoint of the community, for the experience, skills, and capital remain available for other efforts.

From the viewpoint of the concerned public official, a program to encourage many company formations is a relatively low-risk and potentially high-gain effort. It shifts attention and responsibility to the successes and failures, in aggregate, of the many company formation efforts (another actuarial aspect). A program that generates several entrepreneurial formations distributes the political and economic risks over a large number of smaller and less visible points than does the program that is focused on one or two large, expensive, highly visible, long-term projects. Furthermore, a program to encourage many new companies to be formed has a fair likelihood of producing some success early and during any single year of the program, while a very large project takes several years before success or failure can be determined.

5.   Cultural fit. The entrepreneur, even when drawn from a minority or immigrant group, is part of the fabric of the culture in which he is found. The entrepreneur lives close to and is part of the culture of the country and locale. He is attuned to place and custom, and has an intimate awareness of what can and cannot be done with local resources. Unlike the manager of an immigrant industrial plant, the local entrepreneur does not have to be "oriented," taught how to understand the local natives, given language lessons, taught about the local customs.

The development of an industrial complex in an area

To attain the desired characteristics of diversity, innovativeness, and resilience that have been identified with a dynamic economy implies a multiplicity of companies and, by inference, the kind of industrial ecology or environment that facilitates the formation of new companies in answer to opportunities or problems. The factors going into the formation of a single company that have been discussed above provide the basic building blocks that go into the formation of an industrial complex or community, but there are other questions that need to be asked in terms of the "community of companies" as differentiated from the simple aggregation of individual company statistics. One question has to do with the kinds of companies sought. When one goes beyond the obvious kinds of companies that are linked perforce to the presence of local mineral resources or touristic countryside, the choices are quite numerous. What kinds of companies should a community attempt to promote in its midst (or attract to its midst)?

What kinds of companies?

The kinds of companies or economic efforts that are desirable for an area are those that not only bring jobs and income to the region, as has already been pointed out, but those that by their nature will enhance the quality of the area's human capital and its long-term capability to deal with the unknown future. Furthermore, in addition to desirability there is the question of feasibility; the kinds of new ventures that can succeed are those in economic sectors or niches that have ease of entry. The kinds of economic activity that exemplify what may be termed "high-value" companies for a community are often companies that are engaged in high technology — the kinds of companies that are dependent on highly professional and skilled manpower. Many economic developers regard high-technology companies as especially attractive to an area's overall development program because the companies:

1. Utilize and develop products and technologies that may provide the basis for new, growth industries.
2. Provide a community with an employment composition that has much higher than average income and educational levels.
3. Attract a work force that undertakes a large and active role in an area's educational, cultural and social activities.
4. Create a community image that makes the area attractive to other kinds of economic enterprise.
5. Provide employment opportunities that attract and retain an area's college-educated, technically and professionally trained citizens.

The process

A number of studies of high-technology, industrial complexes in the United States provide us with some useful clues as to the way the process of development of an industrial complex occurs in the United States. The data even suggest that the process may be generalized to other than technical industrial complexes since they are primarily dependent on the individual company-formation process, which has been found to be similar in many kinds of industry and different countries and cultures. The technical-company-formation process in an area can be categorized into three phases:

1. A period in which the first one to four technical companies are formed, quasi-randomly.
2. A period of accumulation and incubation in which technical companies are formed at a rate of approximately one per year.

3. A period of accelerated and sustained growth in which technical companies are formed at a rate of approximately two or more per year.

The first phase: the first company formed   The first technical company formed in a local area can be considered as an almost random event, for seldom can the first formation be explained in terms of calculated decisions made by an "economic man" acting rationally. In almost every case, the first technical company is distant from its markets, and there is little chance that its support services are available in a community that has not had previous experience with technical companies. In many of the instances studied, it was found that the first company founded survived in the area for decades despite the lack of important services and immediate markets. Whether or not the first technical company in an area survives is a function of a number of factors, such as whether or not the founder-manager is far better than average as a manager or technical professional, whether or not the company has a product or service sufficiently unique and salable to give the company a temporary monopoly in the marketplace, whether or not the company has access to financing and support services, and whether or not they are locally available. Often the first company survives through obtaining enough immediate sales and trade credit to make it independent of local financial support, and through supplying its own support services—even as marginal operations that take away from its profits.

The quasi-random, first company type of formation may be repeated with a second, third, and fourth company, each completely independent or even oblivious of the existence of previous companies. After the first companies are formed and have survived, however, their very presence in the community becomes a definite positive factor in subsequent technical-company formations. In many cases, the first companies become sources of entrepreneurs for subsequent company formations through spin-off. Furthermore, each existing company enhances the credibility of company formation to others within the company and community. As personal displacements are experienced by employees of those dealing with the first companies, nascent entrepreneurs are triggered to take action. The presence of other technical companies makes founding a company a realistic and credible alternative.

The second phase: accumulation and incubation   As the number of technical companies formed in the community increases, the technical company-formation process loses its random nature and enters a phase of accumulation and incubation. There is the beginning of a technical labor pool, the market for supporting services grows and begins to attract manufacturers' representatives, and the area gains warehousing of needed supplies. Supporting services are exchanged among the technical companies in the city, and local providers of professional services become "educated" to the special character and needs of technical industries.

During the second phase of development, because of its growing technical character, an area often attracts industry. A large corporate division, added to the accumulating number of locally generated companies, provides considerable impetus to the creation of a local technical labor pool, and the attraction of suppliers and services. The in-migrant division then becomes, in turn, another source of potential entrepreneurs. Community factors play a contributory role in the overall development process, particularly during the second phase. The presence of a local university is an amenity that acts to attract and retain technical workers. Many corporations consider the presence of a university as one of their major location criteria for a technical division. Cultural amenities, such as theater, music, and entertainment, play a similar role to that of a university. Local facilities for education are highly important as a family attraction. All of a community's special attractions create a community with an intellectual profile that tends to attract technical entrepreneurs and the key manpower resources they must collect.

Areas that have high tourist attraction value (i.e., the "sunshine" states, coastal resorts, etc.) have an advantage in attracting and retaining potential entrepreneurs, technical professionals, and corporate divisions from other areas. Familiarity with an area resulting from many years of attracting tourists provides a "pull" on all kinds of industries, particularly on the "footloose" industries— those not tied to local natural resources or transportation services. High-technology companies are in the footloose category. The primary resource in a technical activity is the technical professional work force. Given the attractive community as a location, the company experiences less trouble in bringing the necessary resources to the location.

The third phase: sustained growth   The number of technical companies accumulates in an area, and a point is reached in which the technical-company-formation process begins to sustain itself. The number of technical-company-formations rises from one year to two or more a year. Services formerly maintained as marginal operations within the companies are now spun-off to provide efficient services to a community of companies. The more companies in the community, the greater the number of sources for potential spin-off and the greater the increase in the formation rate.

The time required to reach the third phase and the strength of its thrust is dependent on the way the earlier phases of technical-company-formation in a community have developed. The greater the variety of technical companies in the community, the greater the apparent strength of the third phase. When a community develops as a technical industry area clustered around a single specialty, the development is more limited. A single specialty area may create more jobs than other areas, but it is less resilient to shifts and variations in the marketplace.

Making it happen

Can entrepreneurship be deliberately made to happen in a community? What can we affect in the process of eliciting and developing and even attracting entrepreneurial behavior in a community? What can be done to generate the entrepreneurial events that might be a key to the development of a self-sustaining, developmental process in a community and in a region?

Some of the elements that might be included in entrepreneurial development programs include the following:

Actions to attract small and diverse companies to a region   New companies form more readily from small companies rather than large companies. Furthermore, smaller firms gain real advantage from small concessions, while larger firms must be given very large concessions. Smaller companies also generate entrepreneurs.

Programs to generate new company formation   It is possible to provide potential entrepreneurs with experiences that will make the company-forming act more credible to them.

Programs to provide the industrial "ecology" that will enable new companies to form and survive   These can include: (1) programs for educating the financial community in the risks and characteristics of new, small companies and in the requirements of different industries; (2) the development and fielding of substitutes for the various factors and services only available in very large, well-established communities (an example could be governmental support for a network of excellent manufacturers' representatives as a substitute for the market opportunities of a larger community); (3) special efforts to attract the kinds of support services to a community that make company start-up less costly and company survival easier to achieve—machine shops, plating services, blueprinting, etc.; (4) transportation support services; (5) incubator industrial facilities with low rentals and various services on an as-needed basis.

Action experiments

There is a very useful function to be played by a program of action experiments (i.e., demonstration efforts that are "instrumented" for measurement of results) in entrepreneurship. The translation of knowledge into useful action can be greatly facilitated by use of a socio-economic equivalent of the engineering test of new developments or what the English refer to as "trials." Too many programs have been fielded on the basis of very plausible ideas that have not been submitted to the far less costly (in both economic and political terms) process of trials. The trial process serves to test the feasibility of a program, and it can be an important means for obtaining the feedback of data that will enable the developing organization to improve the program before it is finally fielded. Some examples of action experiments relevant to entrepreneurship and local economic development are the following:

1. Design of a standby program for the encouragement of company formations following major displacements. Much as the Red Cross has a standby capability for the saving of lives in the event of an emergency, it is possible to preplan efforts that would go into effect when a major displacement occurs due to such events as the closing of a military base, a major cutback in an aerospace contract, or a major layoff in a large industrial plant.

2. Design and test of a "return home" program in which skilled and professional emigrants from an area are encouraged to return home to start new companies.

3. Design and test of university-related programs to field new technology through the spin-off of companies.

4. Design and test of a series of ethnic entrepreneurship programs that make use of the available data rather than non-data-based ideas, including efforts to make the company-formation act credible to those subsections of an ethnic group that are most likely to respond successfully.

5. Design and test of a series of experiments aimed at spinning off government and industrial scientists and engineers with "pieces" of technology that have already been invested in by the government through its many R & D programs for mission-oriented agencies.

6. Development and test of a program to orient key sources of funds to support company formations.

1. Jane Jacobs, *The Economy of Cities* (New York: Random House, 1969).
2. Dudley Dillard, *Economic Development of the North Atlantic Community* (Prentice-Hall, 1967).
3. Jacobs.
4. Quoted in E. F. Schumacher, *Small is Beautiful* (London: Blond & Briggs, 1973).
5. *New York Times*, 26 May 1975.
6. Jacobs.
7. Joseph A. Schumpeter, *The Theory of Economic Development*, Harvard Economic Studies (Cambridge: Harvard University, 1934).
8. Jonathan Hughes, *The Vital Few* (New York: Houghton Mifflin, 1965).
9. Dickerson and Kawaja in: Irving Pfeffer, ed., *The Financing of Small Business* (New York: The Macmillan Company, 1967).

Concepts of Public-Private Cooperation

Harold Wolman and Larry Ledebur

Cities are changing in their economic functions and characteristics. Increasingly it is apparent that government's images of cities must also change. The concept of an autonomous business sector acting in pursuit of its own immediate goals, and a public sector with discrete responsibilities and objectives, no longer works well; it no longer mirrors the emergent realities and interdependencies of the economic and social environment of the city.

Business executives are increasingly recognizing that the success of their enterprises depends, to some degree, on the condition of the city in which they operate. Some businesses have responded by seeking ways to work toward improving their environments, others have chosen to escape their conditions through relocation. Meanwhile, public officials are coming to understand that the welfare of the city is integrally related to the health of its economic base, and that their capacity to respond effectively to urban problems depends in no small way on the interest and involvement of the local business sector in the resources it commands.

Accompanying this increasing, mutual recognition of interdependency is the quest for organizational forms: models and processes through which mutual interests can be translated into programmatic responses to the problems and opportunities of the emerging city.

The concept of public-private sector cooperation—engaging the private sector and its resources in cooperative responses to the problems of cities—has gained currency among those concerned with urban conditions and policy. However, while the idea has in-

Reprinted with permission from Management Information Service Reports, vol. 12, no. 1 (Washington, D.C.: International City Management Association, January 1980).

herent appeal to policy makers and urban practitioners, there is a great deal of ambiguity in the concept of partnership or cooperation, and in the manner in which this form of public-private relationship can become practice rather than simply exhortation designed to rally and enlist business leadership and cities. There is a need, therefore, to reach beyond the rhetoric to a careful evaluation of both the concept and the efforts to implement this model of private-public sector relations in cities.

Forms of public-private interaction

Cooperation, or partnership, is but one of several possible forms of interaction between public and private sector institutions in a city. As we shall see, in many ways it is the most ambiguous form of interaction. To delineate the meaning of cooperation, and to distinguish it from other forms of public-private sector interaction, it is useful to place the issue in this broader perspective. Below are models of the various forms of interaction.

Laissez-faire   In this form of interaction the public sector permits the private sector to pursue its activities with as little government interaction (regulations, controls, etc.) as possible. The government and business attend to their own functions, and the public sector accepts the resulting pattern of market induced economic activity. In short, the public sector assumes that this laissez-faire approach will produce the best solution or greatest net benefits for society.

Privatization   Here the public sector goes beyond the laissez-faire approach by contracting out some of its functions to the private sector. This assumes public sector functions can be accomplished more efficiently by subjecting their implementation to the discipline of the marketplace.

Promotion   In this model the public sector promotes private sector development in certain areas by providing the preconditions for that development in such areas as the public infrastructure and work force education and training. These preconditions are established under the presumption that they will attract private sector economic activity to the city. No prior agreement with representatives of the business community exists.

Cooperation   The public and private sectors cooperate or act in partnership to achieve a mutually shared goal in this form of interaction. One example would be agreements between the public sector and representatives of the private sector that stipulate if the public sector establishes certain preconditions (e.g., public infrastructure), the business sector will respond in a specified manner.

Inducement   In this arrangement the public sector provides incentives to the private sector to induce private sector behavior that will accomplish public goals. This relationship differs from cooperation, because it does not assume that the public and private sectors share mutual goals. Instead it recognizes that the private sector's primary goal is profit, and attempts to structure circumstances by which the private sector, in pursuing its profit objective, will at the same time accomplish public ends.

Regulation or control   Here the public sector regulates or controls private sector behavior so that it is consistent with public objectives.

Public ownership   In this final form of interaction the public sector assumes and operates some of what, at least in the United States, are commonly assumed to be private sector activities. In effect, this is the converse of the privatization model.

In the historical evolution of cities in the United States, there has been a commitment in ideology, if not practice, to the laissez-faire relationship between the public and private sectors. While exceptions can be cited, generally the issue of the "social accountability" of business in the city did not arise to any significant degree until the latter part of the 1960s. Then the attention of the nation was forcibly drawn to the conditions of the inner city by the urban riots. In many ways the public sector response to the private sector then was to denigrate the social responsibility of business and to use moral suasion to pressure corporate leaders to invest in the deteriorating cores of larger cities.

The response in many parts of the corporate community was defensive. It expressed bewilderment at the challenge to their ethic of social benefits coming out of their endeavors—the ethic that the pursuit of private profit, in the long run, results in public good.[1]

The view that a laissez-faire approach in a competitive economy results in the greatest benefits to society has some basis in economic theory. However, this result depends upon several conditions or assumptions that never exist in a complex society. This outcome could occur in an idealized economy of pure competition through: the interaction of many small firms, with no monopolistic power or influence on competitive prices; full knowledge of firms and consumers; and perfect mobility of labor and other factors of production. In this perfect world any intervention by the public sector could only reduce the aggregate benefits accruing to society, at least those benefits which are priced in the marketplace.

Clearly this idealized world, a figment of economists' theorizing, does not correspond to the realities of urban economics or the national economy. Even if such conditions existed, one consequence would be ongoing geographical reallocations of economic activity, causing some areas to prosper while others experienced economic decline. In fact, if labor and population are not highly mobile, at least in the short run, areas experiencing decline will tend to be characterized by high unemployment, relatively low wages, and poverty.

The laissez-faire imagery is useful as a cautionary influence on what might be believed as a proclivity in the public sector for direct intervention into the local economy to achieve desired public objectives. Cities that recognize the importance of a healthy economic base and the need for a positive climate for business will be careful in considering possible public sector activities that might adversely affect the efficiency and competitiveness of local business enterprises and the perceptions of the business climate held by business leaders.

Nonetheless, there is general acceptance of the view that urban professionals must design positive responses to the deteriorating conditions and emerging needs of their cities. The design and implementation of these programs require the combined resources of the private and public sectors. Thus, the need to identify models and processes which facilitate this type of interaction is clear.

Cooperative partnership versus promotion and inducement

Of the possible forms of relationship between the public and private sectors in cities, promotion, inducement, and cooperation are designed to influence the decisions and behavior of businesses in noncoercive ways (as opposed to regulation or other types of negative controls or incentives). These three interactive models, which build on the primary motivations of the business sector, often are confused. With the current emphasis on cooperation, many programs at the local level that are planned around techniques of promotion or inducement are incorrectly being categorized as partnership arrangements. Below is a more careful look at these three models and their distinctions.

Promotion approach   The promotion approach focuses primarily on the physical conditions of the city and the availability, quality, and price of resources. All these factors are considered to be integral to firms' decisions on where to locate and whether to expand or contract. In this approach city programs focus on upgrading the public infrastructure: roads and forms of transportation, requisite water, sewage and power facilities, and other public services such as fire protection and public safety. In addition, cities are recognizing increasingly that the general quality of the physical environment— the amenities of the city and its ambience—is affecting economic decisions of firms and members of the work force. Measures that attempt to upgrade the quality of the local work force to provide for particular configurations of occupational skills also represent promotion strategies.

Historically, the promotion approach has tended to characterize the economic development strategies and programs of the federal government in the economies of local areas. The primary examples are the Economic Development Administration's public works program, with its promotion of industrial park facilities, and the Community Development Block Grant Program of the Department of Housing and Urban Development.

The particular features of the promotion strategy which distinguish it from those of inducement and cooperative partnership are the emphasis on providing the economic preconditions (facilities and services) for industrial activity and the lack of prior agreement with private sector representatives about their subsequent actions. The objective is to generate circumstances designed to lower firms' production costs in particular sites. Cities expect that the profit making motivations of firms will encourage them then to locate or expand at these sites, or at least not contract or out-migrate.

Inducement approach   The inducement approach accepts the importance and legitimacy of private sector behavior within the American economy, and attempts to channel that behavior toward public sector development goals. This is accomplished not through the imposition of controls but through the structuring of incentives that change the market environment in which private business operates. It is then hoped that private entities, in freely pursuing their own self-interests (i.e., attempting to maximize profits), will simultaneously accomplish public objectives.

The inducement approach is attractive, particularly to economic theorists. Charles Schultze, chairman of President Carter's Council of Economic Advisors, has written:

Market-like arrangements not only minimize the need for coercion as a means of organizing society; they also reduce the need for compassion, patriotism, brotherly love, and cultural solidarity as a motivating force behind social improvements. Harnessing the *base* motive of material self-interest to promote the common goal is perhaps the most important social invention mankind has yet achieved.[2]

Programs that use the inducement approach are designed to attract business to a community through subsidies that lower operating or capital cost. Examples include the multitude of tax subsidies available at state and local levels.

An effective program design based on the use of incentives requires a thorough understanding of private sector behavior. The public sector must be able to predict the private sector's response to the application of various levels of incentives. If it is unable to accurately predict this response, the result may be a windfall to the private sector at the public's expense. For example, if a public subsidy is provided to a business that would have located in the community in any case, then the public subsidy serves no purpose and is merely a windfall to the private business. The inducement approach is not intended as a reward for good behavior. It presupposes that the private sector will *change* its behavior as a consequence of the public inducement.

Unfortunately, the public sector's understanding of private sector behavior is often not subtle enough. In addition to providing inducement subsidies only to those who would not have otherwise engaged in the desired behavior, another problem frequently arises. Private sector actors may find ways to use publicly provided incentives to pursue their self-interest in ways not foreseen by the designers of the incentives and not related to public objectives. The series of scandals associated with the Federal Housing Administration's insured housing programs—programs based to a large extent on providing incentives to private builders, realtors, and lending institutions—are examples of this difficulty.

Cooperative or partnership approach   The cooperation or partnership model is perhaps the most ambiguous of the seven forms of public-private relationships. What are the mutual goals that the public and private sectors share, and through what mechanism or process can they be pursued? Without serious analysis cooperation becomes a mere rhetorical device, an exhortation to both sectors to act in a way which may contravene the interests of one or both sectors.

As we have said, the primary goal of the private sector is to make a profit. This may not be the only goal, but it is surely the basic one, which strongly suggests, at a minimum, that any form of cooperation that implies reduced profits is unlikely to occur except in symbolic ways.

The inducement model indicated that the public sector accepts the motivation for profit and structures incentives so that, while pursuing profit, the private sector will accomplish public objectives as a by-product. The cooperation model, however, suggests a mutuality of goals. What might these mutual goals be?

First, business persons are citizens as well as professionals. An appeal for cooperation to achieve public purposes may succeed if individuals in business personally share the public objective. Second, businesses and corporations require and seek a certain degree of public acceptance. Widely publicized actions to cooperate with public sector goals provide evidence of their social responsibility and good citizenship. Third, the private sector may cooperate with the public sector because one or more of its subgoals may coincide with public sector purposes. Social stability, an educated work force, or infrastructure such as an effective transportation system permitting labor mobility may be subgoals of portions of the private sector because they permit or contribute to the primary goal of profit.

In all three cases, however, private sector cooperation becomes extremely unlikely if one of the consequences is reduced profit. Only an extremely enlightened business person would accept a short-term reduction in profit in exchange for greater long-term returns which might result from cooperation.

What sort of cooperative activity might be expected to emerge from these mutually shared goals? In many cities businesses have demonstrated their good citizenship by making available their expertise to city governments to help them cope with city problems. In some cases this occurs through a loan of employees, in others through creation of special blue ribbon or advisory committees.

City governments have also responded to the needs of business. Governments are moving beyond a passive or regulatory stance to a facilitative approach in which the private sector is viewed as a constituent rather than an adversary. Some cities have established a special office to assist business in finding its way through the city's regulatory maze. In an increasing number of cases cities are actively working with individual businesses to help them meet their needs, particularly for adequate sites and service connections to the sites.

Probably more significant is cooperation in the planning process. This reflects a systemic and structural, cooperative relationship as opposed to the more ad hoc arrangement described above. Many city governments now believe that the well-being of the private sector bears an important relationship to the well-being of the city government and its constituents. Local governments are seeking out the private sector as allies and partners, both in efforts designed specifically to strengthen the city's economies and in the city's ongoing planning process.

The objective of cooperation in the planning process is to assure that major decisions affecting the city's future take into account the needs of the private sector, so that the city is an attractive environment for private economic activity. In this level of interaction the business community is viewed less as one of several interest groups and more as a partner in government. However, since this gives it a substantial advantage over other private groups, there are also potential dangers. There is perhaps a fine line between public-private cooperative activities and dominance by a city's business community, particularly in cities where there is a substantial overlap between the business and political elites.

Finally, the public and private sectors may cooperate in specific joint venture projects. Each agrees to undertake specific activities, and the public sector may agree to assume a portion of the cost. This may resemble the inducement approach, but unlike that approach it involves extensive negotiations and planning for specific projects rather than a more impersonal restructuring of market incentives. Both the old urban renewal program and its successor, the Urban Development Action Grant (UDAG) program, were federal programs designed to bring about this kind of cooperative activity at the local level.

Conclusion

As the above discussion suggests, public-private sector cooperation is full of pitfalls and carries the potential for great frustrations. These frustrations will likely continue if unrealistic expectations are not set aside. Mainly, the primacy of the profit motive in business and the imperatives of bureaucracy in government should be recognized.

Just as the private sector cannot be expected to act altruistically at the expense of profit, so the public sector cannot be expected to eliminate the rules, regulations, and operating characteristics of bureaucracies. Bureaucracies—and public bureaucracies are no exception—are devices for making decisions according to rules. The scope for widespread discretion (e.g., suspension of rules) is extremely limited except at the upper echelons where, perforce, few "on the ground" decisions are made. Clearly public bureaucracies can be made more efficient, but from the perspective of the business person, they will always look entangled in red tape, dilatory, and insensitive to the imperatives of the private sector.

1. Clearly this statement is general and stereotypical. Many corporate enterprises responded by initiating investment and employment programs designed to create jobs in inner cities and to upgrade the quality of life there.

2. Charles C. Schultze, *The Public Use of Private Interest* (Washington, D.C.: Brookings Institution, 1977).

PART 2

Organizing for Economic Development

Community/ Economic Development: Local Responsibilities

Richard Starr

The future substance and, in many cases, continued existence of community and economic development programs will be decided in the very near future. While many officials believe the issues will be decided in Washington (or at the statehouse), in fact, the fate of these programs will be determined at the municipal level. It is not clear whether recent successes in economic and neighborhood development efforts will be enough to save these programs. This is unfortunate, since the need and capacity to perform have never been greater. There is, however, a method of performing a long overdue assessment of current programs with the goal of assuring the continuation of those programs that make sense.

Program evolution

Community and economic development programs have evolved out of the "New Frontier" and "Great Society" eras of the 1960s. This evolution and its implications are often unappreciated by many current practitioners. The predecessor programs (that is, urban renewal, poverty, and model cities programs), contributed a variety of features to the current block grant approach that quite possibly have hampered program effectiveness or at least the ability to respond to changing conditions. While compliance with federally mandated requirements (housing priorities, citizen involvement, neighborhood designation) was laudable in intent, and made sense when the federal government was local government's financial partner, municipalities should reexamine these procedures now that their partner is withdrawing from the relationship.

Reprinted with permission from *Journal of Housing*, published by the National Association of Housing and Redevelopment Officials, July/August 1982.

There are a few carry-over features of the present federally sponsored programs that should be examined in light of the current administration's thrust toward expanded flexibility and diminished resources.

1. *Neighborhood designation.* From the early urban renewal days, there has been a need to designate the area to be aided. This approach, which appears to be continued under the urban enterprise zone concept, may tend to focus scarce resources in areas with the greatest need, but with the least potential for attracting private investment or solving problems.

2. *Program goals.* From the "workable program" through today's block grant submissions, federal programs have encouraged federally conceived and often unrealistic goal statements. This concept has misdirected many local programs and made it extremely difficult to conduct program evaluations. For example, federally encouraged housing goals that ignore population decline, market conditions and, most importantly, diminished federal support programs result in a "no win" situation for local officials.

3. *Citizen participation.* Another carry-over from the 1960s is the concept of citizen participation in program policy and design. Even in situations where the citizen representatives are actually elected, it seems highly unlikely that they will have the expertise and objectivity to deal with diminishing program resources.

There are numerous other examples of how urban programs are ill-prepared to deal with the issues of the 1980s. The capacity to leverage diminishing resources, build off strengths, and maximize federal funds has yet to be developed in many local programs. On the other hand, and a more positive note, the expertise and sophistication of local urban policy makers has been increasing. There is a growing appreciation of how best to use resources and how to conduct public-private urban projects. There is an expanded realization that downtown revitalization, industrial retention or attraction, and neighborhood revitalization will take imaginative programs involving local government assistance and private expertise.

Thus, community and economic development programs enter the 1980s burdened by some obsolete policies and diminishing resources, but with an increasing understanding and appreciation of how to achieve results. Given the obvious urban problems and needs, it is imperative that effective community development programs survive the impending federal retreat.

Perhaps the first step for local government is an objective evaluation of its current urban programs. Program goals, designated neighborhoods and active projects should be reexamined in light of federal policy changes and current local economic conditions. Are local housing goals valid in light of federal financial cutbacks? Can local governments attract private resources to the areas selected? Does job retention or creation deserve a higher priority? Can local officials better leverage block grant funds?

It is possible, but unlikely, that reassessing community and economic programs will result in the continuation of current programs. What is more apt to happen in most cities is that the evaluation will result in programs that are more effective and more suited to current conditions, resources and opportunities.

Perhaps the most important finding of any program evaluation would be that there are a large number of critical urban issues that are not going to be addressed if current community development programs die. The need for cities to have a professional staff dealing with economic, housing, and neighborhood issues has never been more apparent. The new skills and public/private successes need to be increased if cities are to prosper. A municipal agency is needed to maintain the urban data base, identify development opportunities in older neighborhoods, orchestrate public/private development, and provide seed money for urban and job retention projects.

There is a necessary community and economic development function to be conducted in most American cities and it will not occur if current programs go the way of urban renewal, the poverty program and model cities. However, the local agency role must be more than just distributing federal dollars, or the agency will die if that money disappears. The new flexibility that accompanies the rapidly diminishing resources provides local administrators with one last chance to assure the survival of their programs. The key issues include reassessing current programs, developing new concepts and financial resources and gaining support through demonstrated successes.

Program evaluation

Perhaps the most important step for community and economic development officials to take is an immediate, objective evaluation of their current situations and programs. This evaluation should answer the following questions: What are the critical urban and economic issues that presently affect the municipality? What can be done to alleviate or minimize problems with current and anticipated resources? Which opportunities or constraints deserve the focus of limited resources in the immediate future? How can public resources best be leveraged with the private sector?

As a general procedure, the reevaluation should incorporate two factions of the community: the citizen organization that designed the current programs and goals, and representatives of broader municipal leadership. The leadership group should include elected officials, downtown and chamber of commerce members, lenders, major employers and representatives of community-wide organizations. In most cities, these two groups will represent a new coalition and could be named as a mayor's task force to examine and make recommendations on the local community development process. With as much objectivity and as little fault-finding as possible, this task force should perform a two-stage evaluation.

Stage 1 should include an objective evaluation of current program goals, activities and results. This process must include an honest attempt to recognize the economic, political, and legislative factors that have impacted the evolution of all community and economic development programs. Because so many conditions have changed in recent years, the focus of any evaluation should be on that which is actually being accomplished as opposed to why a particular course of action was originally selected.

Stage 2 requires an objective assessment of the municipality's current economic situation, with an emphasis on the opportunity areas that may exist. The experience of the Urban Development Action Grant program demonstrates that it is far easier to leverage public dollars and attract private investment to projects with market potential than to those designed to overcome economic and social problems. The primary opportunity that exists in most every municipality is the potential to maximize existing community development resources. Federal funds are being reduced, but so is the amount of regulation and red tape. In today's money market, block grant funds, loaned to private developers at reduced or no interest rates, can be a tremendous catalyst to private investment. Vacant or under-utilized urban land offers local officials another valuable resource and an opportunity to work with developers on innovative projects. Sale/lease-back arrangements involving municipal property offer still another opportunity to leverage public tax benefits.

The result of the two-stage evaluation should be a more realistic program to deal with traditional community and economic development issues and quite possibly some new approaches more suited for the current national urban policy. Revised approaches could include focusing housing programs on neighborhoods where limited public funds can be maximized or attract the greatest amount of private investment. Neighborhood improvement projects should give priority to areas that will agree to underwrite a portion of the cost or accept a lien that eventually will repay to the city some of the appreciation generated by the public investment.

Some of the current public works aspects of community and economic development programs might be more intelligently financed as part of a municipal bond effort. This approach would free block grant funds for a municipal action grant program (that is, low-interest loans to help local businesses expand), with a pay-back being used to offset all or part of the bond program. In any event, there are undoubtedly many ways that some existing programs could be improved if they are objectively evaluated by someone other than those directly benefiting from the current process.

While almost all community and economic development efforts would benefit from objective evaluation and adjustment to current conditions, this will not assure the long-term survival of the programs. To continue the programs, city staffs will need to expand their roles, find new resources to replace lost federal dollars, and begin to implement innovative financing mechanisms. The expanded role is necessary so that locally sponsored programs become a permanent part of local government activities and so that municipal programs are not entirely dependent on federal funding. Community and economic development must be viewed by elected officials and local citizens as a necessary service.

The most immediate "new" funding source should be a more effective use of remaining community development block grant funds. In most cities, the objective evaluation of existing programs will result in identifying some block grant funds that now are not being effectively employed. An obvious example would include maintaining current levels of effort while using fewer community development dollars and making up the difference through increased leveraging and private participation. This would be accomplished by identifying new sources of funds by tapping corporate, lender, or property owner resources.

Although every city will have to devise its own approach, expanded flexibility in community development funding will facilitate leveraging, particularly opportunities to revolve funds. Consideration should be given to a local action grant program where community development funds are a catalyst for local projects.

Given today's money market, most community development programs should have little difficulty in identifying development projects that would result in employment and tax base expansion. The guaranteed repayment of these community development loans could be used to offset future grant reductions or to repay bonds that have financed other projects.

Additional tax revenues—"new" money—could be generated by using some of the community/economic development resources and tools to attract private development to vacant land. All cities have this very important resource that can be tapped. Real Estate Research Corporation completed a national study for the Department of Housing and Urban Development entitled "Urban Infill."[1] The project evaluated the development potential of vacant land that, for a wide variety of reasons, exists in every urban area. This land is usually fully serviced, surrounded by development but, for some legal, financial, physical, or marketing reason, is undeveloped.

While the RERC research assignment focused on a wide range of local actions that could be employed to attract infill development, two aspects of the project should be of interest to local development officials. The first is that much of the vacant or under-utilized property in many cities is owned by public or semi-public entities. Land assets can be found on the books of tax, highway, park, school, public housing, urban renewal and various other city departments. Changing demographics have left most urban school districts with considerable excess property and, if private institutions are included, the potential resource is even more impressive. When cities inherited a renewal authority or transit company, an often overlooked asset was the real estate that came with the function.

A second, more important aspect is that the public entity involved usually does not have the necessary skills (or possibly the interest) in utilizing its excess property assets. A legitimate objective of the community or economic development department should be to encourage the maximum development of vacant or under-utilized urban property. These land assets offer an opportunity for new development and the creation of jobs and tax resources. In addition, this concept offers community development officials an opportunity to work with sister agencies, use their skills and resources, and to share with them in the rewards. An aggressive community development agency should be able to (1) work with public officials (mayor and council) to identify excess public and semi-public vacant or under-utilized land resources; (2) obtain excess public real estate through donation, option, or purchase at fair market value if necessary; (3) improve the value of the acquired real estate through assemblage, capital improvements, zoning, or financial development assistance; and (4) achieve the desired development of the property through the sale, lease or joint venture approach that replenishes any community development funds expended in the process and, in most cases, results in a net profit for the agency.

Perhaps the most important criterion for survival in a less federally dominated environment will be that of successful projects. While many previous project activities have had federal agency and local political appeal, they have existed only as long as the federal funds continued to flow. If local programs can accomplish hard community and economic development objectives, cities can get local private long-term support.

There is, and will continue to be, a legitimate community and economic development function for local government. Each city will have to decide how it will carry out this activity and which department will perform these functions. City assets such as staff, land, dollars, taxes, improvements, and controls should be viewed as potential public investments. The local development entities that get a return on their investments, adapt to new conditions, and produce will survive and, indeed, may even prosper in the 1980s.

1.   The executive summary of *Urban Infill: Its Potential as a Develop-* *ment Strategy* is reprinted in this book (see page 102).

Setting Up Shop
for Economic
Development

Ruth Knack, James J. Bellus, Patricia Adell

Introduction

Deciding what form an economic development organization should take—a hot issue right now—is a relatively new problem. Economic development used to be primarily the province of the local chamber of commerce, perhaps with some facts and figures supplied by a small economic development office within the municipal planning office. In the late 1950s, federally funded urban renewal offices took the lead in organizing development projects, which, throughout the next two decades, were almost exclusively real estate projects.

The connection between development and jobs strengthened some during the Model Cities era of the late 1960s, but the work of retaining and attracting the big industrial job producers was more often a state than a local responsibility. In the mid-1960s, the advent of the U.S. Economic Development Administration spurred the creation of economic development committees, and the Community Services Administration began to fund neighborhood development corporations. Other nonprofit corporations were formed to take advantage of Small Business Administration programs. Downtown business interests formed their own development corporations.

Philadelphia may have been the first city to establish a nonprofit corporation concerned with the economic development of the entire city, and a lot of places are looking to it as a model now. Today, some 50 citywide economic development corporations are listed in the directory published by the National Council for Urban Eco-

Reprinted with permission from vol. 49, no. 9, October 1983 issue of *Planning.* Copyright 1983 by the American Planning Association, 1313 E. 60th Street, Chicago, Illinois 60637. Ms. Knack wrote the introductory material; Mr. Bellus wrote on St. Paul; and Ms. Adell wrote on Philadelphia.

nomic Development. Some of these groups evolved from Model Cities agencies. The Dayton City-Wide Development Corporation is an example. Others are creations of a local chamber of commerce or, like the Philadelphia Industrial Development Corporation, of the chamber and the city government. Some concentrate on financing and land development for industry, as PIDC did in the beginning. Later, it broadened its focus to include financial assistance for commercial enterprises—an emphasis of many of the newer corporations as well.

Some of the corporations have an extremely close relationship with the city government (the Baltimore Economic Development Corporation, BEDCO, for one). Others are governed by boards completely composed of private sector representatives. A mixture may be more typical. For example, a new economic development commission in the small city of Aurora, Illinois, is sponsored equally by the city and the chamber of commerce. The salary of the single staff member is shared by both, with office space provided by the chamber. The nine-member board is appointed by the mayor, four from a list provided by the chamber of commerce, and five from a list drawn up by the city.

Although all the quasi-public corporations pride themselves on their no-strings approach to development, evidently this stance is not enough to allay private-sector frustration entirely. Recently, some 25 big corporations in Philadelphia each agreed to chip in $50,000 a year to support a new, completely private, economic development corporation, the Greater Philadelphia First Corporation. According to a planner in the Delaware Valley Regional Planning Commission, the new group grew out of the dissatisfaction of those who felt that economic development groups in the metropolitan area were working at cross purposes and that private contributions were not being invested according to a clearly defined strategic plan. The new corporation, which is directed by Ralph Widner, will fund specific projects in response to proposals by civic organizations and quasi-public agencies. Its board includes a representative of PIDC.

Staying put   At the opposite end of the spectrum from the private groups are those economic development departments that determine to remain an integral part of city government. The model in this case is Portland, Oregon, which in 1973 merged five bureaus and commissions into one umbrella agency, the Office of Planning and Development (which has since been disbanded). Other examples are St. Louis, which recently reorganized its planning department to include economic development, and Oakland, California, which in 1979 merged its community development and employment and training offices into a super-agency—the Office of Economic Development and Employment.

In the view of Alan Gregerman, research director of the National Council for Urban Economic Development (CUED) in Washington, both options—the strengthened city department and the quasi-public corporation—have their own strengths and limitations. "The form that works best in a particular city," he suggests, "is a function of many factors, including community size, economic circumstances, local development objectives, and the level of commitment of public and private sectors to economic improvement. In big cities, he adds, "it's reasonable to have a number of different economic development organizations—as long as they communicate and complement each other."

Gregerman believes the public approach works well in cities where the local government has given a high priority to economic development and the private sector is already actively involved—as it is in St. Paul. In contrast, he says, a quasi-public corporation may be more effective in communities where economic development is only one of many priorities competing for scarce public dollars, or where the private sector is uneasy about working directly with local government. (To put it more frankly, in a city where clout rules, a corporation, which can often bypass the city council, may get more done.)

Increasingly, Gregerman notes, communities are choosing the quasi-public route. He sees no reason to change, however, if an effective economic development department is already in place. In short, if it isn't broken, don't fix it.

The organizational issue came to a head in Chicago, where a business-sector advisory group, Chicago United, pointing to Philadelphia as a model, was pushing for the creation of a strong, new quasi-public entity. However, Robert Mier, who was appointed economic development commissioner by mayor Harold Washington, expressed opposition to the idea of putting too much power in the hands of a private body. Mier, a planner, was the director of the Center for Urban Economic Development at the University of Illinois at Chicago. His confirmation by the city council, it should be noted, is [at the time of writing] by no means a sure thing in the city's politically turbulent atmosphere. Some business leaders have expressed fears that his interests are too slanted toward the neighborhoods, to the neglect of downtown.

"The major question," says Mier, "is the degree to which economic development gets privatized. The city must retain responsibility for policy making, and it must remain accountable for its use of public resources."

New direction   Mier does believe, however, that there is a place for an implementation organization "to take on things when the market fails." He has proposed, in fact, that the city create a new industrial development corporation—an idea that Mayor Washington made part of his platform. But Mier would make the new body responsible to the economic development commission rather than remaining independent, as Chicago United would prefer.

Rather than strengthening the private side, Mier wants to beef up the city's economic development planning—pulling development and employment training together in one agency along the lines of Oakland or San Antonio, both of which he often refers to as models. "In the past," he says, "economic development in American cities meant real estate development. I think we seduced ourselves into thinking that if we could solve the land problem, we could solve the economic development problem. What we ended up with is economic development in cities that were good at real estate development. What's needed now is to put jobs back at the center."

St. Paul: we kept it in city government

Editor's note: This first-person account of St. Paul's Department of Planning and Economic Development was prepared by its head, James J. Bellus.

In St. Paul, we believe that economic development can best be accomplished by an agency that is an integral part of city government. Our proof is a track record that compares favorably to that of any private or nonprofit development agency.

In the early 1970s, the situation was different. Efforts by local government to spur development in the depressed inner city were hampered by in-fighting among agencies, lack of political leadership, and an inefficient government structure. Development functions were split among three agencies, the Housing and Redevelopment Authority, and the offices of planning and community development. None of the three had the authority or the wherewithal to deal with the problems caused by a stagnating local economy. (With a population of 270,000, St. Paul is the smaller, and somewhat more industrial, of the Twin Cities. The Minneapolis–St. Paul metropolitan area has a million residents.)

Immediately after his 1976 election, Mayor George Latimer began to push the creation of an umbrella agency that would merge the city's economic development functions. A year later, the Department of Planning and Economic Development was formed. PED operates with five divisions: community development, housing, business redevelopment, downtown development, and planning.

In the six years since then, PED has been widely recognized for its development successes, starting with a downtown project, the $100 million Town Square office-retail complex. Through PED's efforts, St. Paul ranks fourth in the nation in overall volume of Urban Development Action Grants (UDAGs) received, with $50.8 million awarded for 15 grants. In 1981 the city ranked first in the total amount of revitalization grants and loans to small businesses. In five years, we have provided $111 million to small businesses and helped create or retain over 3,000 jobs.

During this time, PED has shepherded through numerous other commercial development projects, hospital expansions, and neighborhood office developments. A major source of funds is the city's tax-exempt revenue bond program, which also has netted $218 million for new housing development since 1977. In addition, PED has financed the rehabilitation of more than 6,800 housing units in low-income neighborhoods and aided commercial development with such projects as the Selby Avenue business revitalization program. This year, using community development block grants and city tax funds, PED established a $2.25 million self-help fund, the Neighborhood Partnership Program, to which neighborhood groups can apply for development projects.

We're responsible   We think this kind of activity can take place only when city departments are working cooperatively and when they are fully aware of the city's total economic, housing, commercial, and recreation needs. A private or quasi-public development agency is less likely to be responsive to public sentiment and to the opinions of major decision makers than we are. One reason is that city government staff members have easier access to their mayors and city councils. They have the advantage of working closely with other city departments and they are more involved with the citizen participation process. A city agency has a vested interest in following the development goals established by the city's comprehensive plan. Because citizens are involved, development does not take place in isolation.

There are drawbacks, of course. Bureaucracy can be a problem, and public disclosure requirements can cause delays. But corporations have their own bureaucracies, and they also suffer from the human inadequacies that cause delays in any type of organization. Nonprofit development agencies have their own hierarchies of staffers who must sign off on various decisions. They, too, are accountable to boards and community groups.

Whenever possible, we try to refine our procedures to speed up development. For example, we recently received permission from the city council to place options on property without holding a public hearing—allowing us to enter into negotiations with potential developers without setting off a speculative flurry. Final acquisition of a site does require public review, but by then the details are unlikely to change.

An often-heard complaint is that government has too little expertise to handle complicated development financing. The key here is for government development agencies to hire people who are motivated, inquisitive, creative, and flexible, and who can relate both to the needs of the public and the goals of the private developer—

just as a private or nonprofit entity would have to do. These people can and do exist in government. But they must be sought out; trained in real estate, financing, and tax law; and given sufficient staff support to make the best use of their talents.

PED inherited a staff of 300 when its three predecessor agencies were merged. Since then, it has grown much leaner—today's staff is about half that number—as a result both of city budget reductions and a conscious effort to operate more efficiently. One reason that the department can operate with a smaller staff is that it works cooperatively with other agencies. A major project currently, for instance, is Energy Park, a $250 million venture of PED and the St. Paul Port Authority. The project will include an "energy technology center," primarily to house small, energy-related businesses and to be managed by the Control Data Corporation. With the aid of a $50 million revenue bond issue, PED is financing and coordinating the construction of 950 housing units on the site. In addition, the city secured two UDAGs to provide the necessary infrastructure.

A total approach   In sum, we feel that by combining housing and commercial financing, planning, zoning, and small business programs in one agency, PED is able to take a total development approach to any area of the city. For example, in Lowertown, the historically significant warehouse district east of the downtown core, PED, working with the foundation-backed Lowertown Redevelopment Corporation, is providing revenue bond financing, UDAGs, and technical assistance for a variety of renewal projects. At the same time, it is working with the artists who are being priced out of the area's lofts—providing one group with a Neighborhood Partnership Program grant to buy a warehouse and convert it into cooperative housing and work space.

It is interesting to note how closely our activities parallel those of quasi-public organizations. Technically, we also have the ability to handle industrial development, although in St. Paul that activity has been left to the port authority. Of course, not all governments are set up to get maximum performance from a public development agency. For them, a private, or quasi-public, development corporation may be the best bet. However, when a city has good political leadership and key staff members have the foresight and acumen to understand the value of good, city-controlled development, then a public development agency should be the choice.

Philadelphia: we set up a separate corporation

Editor's note: This description of the Philadelphia Industrial Development Corporation was prepared by its director of program development, Patricia Adell.

Twenty-six years ago, the Greater Philadelphia Chamber of Commerce and the city itself jointly established a nonprofit corporation, the Philadelphia Industrial Development Corporation, to find ways of creating and retaining jobs, and of improving the city's tax base. PIDC's initial strategy was to help finance industrial enterprises and to develop and market city-owned industrial land. It has since expanded its focus to include financing and marketing assistance to commercial interests, and it has become recognized as one of the nation's most successful economic development agencies. Since 1960, it has settled 1,758 projects with a capital investment of over $1.5 billion; over 175,000 jobs have been created and retained as a result.

We think its success is due in large measure to the fact that the corporation is a collaborative effort of the public and private sectors.

For one thing, its structure is more effective and flexible than the alternative—an economic development department that is an integral part of city government. PIDC's policies are set by a 32-member board, composed of representatives from the public and private sectors. The city itself has seven ex officio seats. A third of the board changes every year and is selected by a nominating committee. A 17-member executive committee meets biweekly; the full board meets quarterly. We have found that the public-private board composition has encouraged the public sector to adopt development policies favorable to business expansion and retention. Even more important, the formal organization provides a platform for public-private interaction.

More freedom   Moreover, our implementation powers are significantly less restrained by the legal strictures of the city charter than a city department's would be. Thus, PIDC, through its subsidiaries, can acquire, develop, sell, and lease land; provide financing through tax-exempt bonds and mortgages; act as a conduit for direct loans from private lending institutions; and put together a variety of financial packages. We have enough flexibility in managing and investing our financial resources to meet the needs of new and growing businesses—avoiding most of the red tape often associated with public-sector bureaucracies. Because project-by-project citizen review is usually not required, we can act much faster than a public agency, although, of course, we are governed by the lending and development policies approved by the public sector and our own board. As a quasi-public entity, we have an easier time gaining the trust of private business than our public counterparts, and we are not as directly affected by political changes.

We can provide a wide range of development assistance—from selling and improving land through our land banking program, to marketing and negotiating the sale or lease of publicly owned properties. As a corporation, we have the flexibility to negotiate the sale of property directly, or to open the sale to bids by qualified developers. Whereas the public sector often is required to accept the lowest bid, we can select a developer who demonstrates financial capability, high-quality design, and experience. Finally, our implementation capabilities are enhanced by a variety of subsidiaries and affiliates, including the Philadelphia Authority for Industrial Development (PAID), a state-authorized, tax-exempt mortgage program; and the PIDC Financing Corporation (PIDC-FC) and the PIDC Local Development Corporation (PIDC-LDC), mechanisms for low-interest, second-mortgage financing.

Our involvement in the 34-acre waterfront redevelopment area known as Penn's Landing is one example of how we work. PIDC is responsible for marketing and developing the landfill site for offices and housing. That means selecting developers and working with the U.S. Army Corps of Engineers and other nonlocal agencies to get the necessary transportation links and to line up environmental permits.

One-stop shop   In effect, we have created a one-stop shop for companies interested in coming into the city or expanding their current operations. As a quasi-public corporation, we've been able to integrate implementation powers with the responsibilities of research, planning, and marketing, and even acting as ombudsman—for instance, by pushing for building code enforcement and more police protection for a company fearful about expanding in a rough neighborhood.

We can also respond quickly in an area where timing is crucial. Manufacturing firms cannot afford to hold off on production and expansion plans while an agency requests various public approvals. We can put together a tailormade loan package, using a combination of local and state funds. In turn, this financing can be used to leverage private mortgage and loan money. The revolving fund used to write down the cost of land sold through our land bank was capitalized with community development block grant money, and the block grants are a mainstay of the second-mortgage loan program, a special, inner-city loan program, and a technology program for start-up firms.

The public-private structure maximizes the powers of both sides. Since the municipal debt ceiling is not affected by debts created by the corporation, the city is protected from financial risk. At the same time, the corporation can draw upon the city's power of eminent domain and its zoning and taxing powers.

Part of the reason that we can do all these things is that we can recruit and hire competent and experienced people without the restrictions of the city's civil service system. Since the beginning, we have offered salaries that are competitive with the private sector—an important incentive in attracting high-caliber staff members. Over the years, we've grown from a tiny staff of three to our present complement of 42 professionals with a yearly budget of over $2 million.

Our legal status as a tax-exempt entity allows us to accept donations from corporations and business groups. On the public side, we have covered some of our administrative expenses through the Economic Development Administration's 302(a) planning funds. In addition, we've received some state and city grants and at various times have contracted with the city, through our subsidiary, the PIDC Development Management Corporation, to perform specific services. PIDC also can generate its own funds through loan settlement, processing, and application fees.

We think the quasi-public corporation, with its legal flexibility and combination of public and private resources, offers the broadest range of powers and the strongest opportunity for coordination between the public and private sectors. Although independent to some degree, it also recognizes its responsibility to both sides—to the private sector in creating a favorable business climate and to the public sector in creating job opportunities and improving the city's tax base.

Organizing and Operating a Development Department

Edward deLuca

How do you keep companies from moving out of your city? It's not an easy job. There are no pat answers. What works with one company may not work with another. Economic conditions change and require new solutions.

Because no one community is the best location for all businesses, it is necessary to develop a game plan which will enable your department to keep and attract those companies which meld best with your community's advantages. Following are ten suggestions on how to establish, strengthen and expand the functions of your development department.

Organize and set goals

Good organization is essential to the efficient operation of any development department—it forces you to think how you can operate best. Figure 1 shows a suggested functional organization chart. The activities under each function serve as a checklist, but they could change as they are completed or no longer are necessary.

The development department acts as a catalytic agent, as a prodder, as a burr. It doesn't try to do everything itself. It stimulates ideas and enlists help from others. The planning department and the urban redevelopment authority are essential to the operation of a strong economic development program, but the more organizations and agencies that are brought into the program, the stronger the program will be. It is important that the activities of all agencies involved are coordinated—struggle for turf will weaken the

Reprinted with permission from the October 1978 issue of *Commentary*, a quarterly magazine published by the National Council for Urban Economic Development.

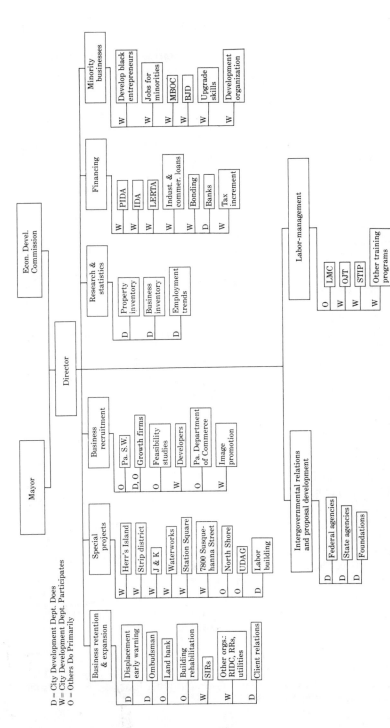

Figure 1. City development functional organization chart.

program. There's ample credit for all. Keep others informed and let them share the limelight.

Figure 1 is coded D, W, and O. These letters indicate those activities which the city development department primarily does (D), those in which city development participates (W), and those which are primarily done by others (O).

Develop basic economic data

Economic data is needed to determine trends, and the city's strong and weak points. Every professional staff person in Pittsburgh's City Development Department has a copy of the basic economic data in a ring binder for ready reference. This data book contains information on population characteristics, labor force, employment, wages, manufacturing, wholesaling, retailing, selected services and utilities.

Having the city's strong points at hand is particularly useful when trying to convince companies to stay or relocate to Pittsburgh.

Our analyses indicate that companies with these characteristics are best suited to Pittsburgh: (1) high labor skills; (2) high wages; (3) labor intensive; (4) fabrication rather than assembly; (5) non-standard or specialty manufacturing; (6) varying and unusual requirements; (7) need for fast transportation of products; (8) need for customer visits to plant; (9) proximity to suppliers; (10) items manufactured to customer specifications; (11) unusual utility requirements; and (12) unusual service requirements.

We feel that small companies, new companies, minority companies, companies servicing the health and medical field, the printing industry, metalworking companies, research and development organizations, and service type companies can make a good profit in Pittsburgh.

Obtain visibility and cooperation

If companies don't know that you're around, or how you can help them, you're not going to accomplish much.

We wanted to contact Pittsburgh manufacturers but could find no comprehensive list of them. We compiled an industrial directory which lists 594 Pittsburgh manufacturing firms alphabetically and by category. The name of the chief executive, the company's address, telephone number and the number of employees are all listed.

We were then able to mail the companies a one-page questionnaire asking about their plans and offering to help them. The questionnaire was accompanied by an introductory letter from Mayor Caliguiri. We received 42 requests for help. About three months later, we sent another questionnaire inquiring about their needs for skill training, again with a cover letter from the mayor. In the past year, every manufacturer has received at least four communications from us. Most of them now know who we are, what we do, and where we can be reached. Files have been set up for the 107 companies with which we have worked to date.

Other methods used to increase the department's visibility include:

1. Organized a meeting on financing and federal aid attended by local bank and Economic Development Administration (EDA) officials. Now we know the banks and they know us.
2. Contacted individual industrial realtors and followed up with group meetings. We now have their trust and work confidentially with them.
3. Visited other organizations involved in development and invited their cooperation. One of these organizations, the Allegheny Conference on Community Development, subsequently underwrote the costs of a day-long seminar attended by more than 100 people. Front page newspaper headlines and extensive radio and television coverage resulted.
4. At our request the Chamber of Commerce organized an economic development committee composed of eight top business executives. Some of the things this committee has done, free of charge, include inspecting vacant multi-story factory buildings and recommending potential reuses; designing and printing 20,000 attractive brochures about Pittsburgh; creating a work plan for the Labor-Management Council and helping to obtain a grant for funding from the U.S. Department of Labor; and analyzing proposed legislation on tax abatement for rehabilitation, expansion, and construction of commercial and industrial buildings.

We also made talks to civic organizations, presented our economic development program to the city council, and appeared on radio and television programs. Most businessmen and community organizations now know us. As a result, companies and people come to us for help, and we know where to go to get help.

Establish land banks

Land (sites and/or buildings) is one of the most important factors in urban economic development. Without land, you're dead. Like most older cities, Pittsburgh is "land short." In our department's short existence, we've been frustrated by our inability to furnish suitable sites for several companies. Surveys conducted in several cities cite the lack of land as the biggest single factor in losing companies. Looking down the road a year or two, our special project activities should ease this problem.

If you refer back to Figure 1, all of the special projects, except labor building, involve acquiring and improving land or buildings for future use. Under research and statistics, the property inventory and business inventory functions involve continuous searching for industrial land and buildings, cataloging and coding the information by size, and keeping it up to date for quick reference and use.

Money for land acquisition and preparation is hard to come by. Federal and state low-cost loans to buy land would help tremendously. These loans would be repaid as the land is sold. Until some legislation is passed, we're exploring a novel idea to help us. We searched for companies with undeveloped acreage in Pittsburgh and have found a few. We proposed to one company that it sell its 300 acres to the city for one dollar. The city will put in the infrastructure and prepare the land for use. As the property is sold, the company will be reimbursed at a price per acre to be agreed upon now. To our pleasant surprise, the company agreed to consider this. Our bait, of course, was that the company would be free from paying taxes when the title is transferred. (Incidentally, the tax millage on land in Pittsburgh is double the millage on improvements.)

Know your financing resources

For quick and accurate reference we compiled a financial handbook for use by the development department staff. There are three sections to the book—local, state, and federal.

In the local section we outline our Commercial and Industrial Loan Program, the Local Economic Revitalization Tax Assistance (LERTA) Act, our Industrial Revolving Fund, and the Allegheny County Industrial Development Act. In the state section, the operation of the Pennsylvania Industrial Development Authority (PIDA) is explained, as are the Pennsylvania Revenue and Mortgage Act (revenue bonds) and the state site preparation grants. In the federal section, reference is made to SBA financing, grants and loans, HUD programs, particularly Urban Development Action Grants (UDAG), the Department of Labor and Appalachian Regional Commission grants.

There is also a reminder that Pennsylvania has *no* tax on machinery, equipment and tools used in manufacturing.

Consider building rehabilitation

One of the greatest attractions of the suburbs is the industrial park. The cities, on the other hand, have hidden assets in their multi-story, older industrial buildings, many of which are vacant. With rehabilitation, many of these buildings can furnish conveniently located space at low cost.

Naturally, a detailed inspection and analysis of the buildings must be made to determine the economic feasibility of converting these structures into modern operating facilities. Removal of non-bearing columns and walls can provide more open space. Efficient freight and passenger elevators can be installed. Modern plumbing facilities can replace outmoded ones. New windows, cosmetic treatment, truck docks, and provision of off-street loading and parking are other items to be considered.

Developers usually look for about an 18 to 20 percent return on rehabilitated buildings because of the potential risk of running into unconsidered factors. If the physical structure is sound, however, rehabilitated buildings cost considerably less than new construction. We call these rehabs vertical industrial parks. As we did with land, we are going to search the city for vacant industrial structures which appear to be economically feasible for conversion and attempt to buy them for one dollar, with further payment after conversion and sale or lease.

Develop minority entrepreneurs and jobs

Too much lip service and not enough action has been given to helping minorities. No city can remain healthy and strong without strengthening this sector in its economy. It must be given special and continuous help so that entrepreneurs and contractors can be strengthened, expanded and started, so that skills can be upgraded, so that jobs can be found for the unemployed, so that necessary financing can be provided.

We are developing a Minority Enterprise Small Business Investment Corporation (MESBIC), a revolving loan fund, and a neighborhood revitalization program. We are going to rehabilitate with an EDA grant the building owned by the Business and Job Development Corporation (BJD) to make it economically self-sufficient. We will inventory minority businesses, push for allocation of purchases from minorities, and explore business opportunities.

Obtain federal grants

The financial facts of life in most cities are such that it's necessary to obtain federal grants to develop and carry on a strong and meaningful economic development program. As far as economic development is concerned, an important agency is the Economic Development Administration (EDA) of the U.S. Department of Commerce. However, HUD and the Department of Labor are now intensely interested in economic development.

The Washington plethora of programs, changes, rules, conditions, and explanations requires continual search, study and analysis. In our department a staff member works almost full-time on *trying* to stay abreast of the federal printing machine, interpreting what he reads, deciding what programs, grants or aids will help us most, gathering the necessary back-up information to write the stories which Washington wants, conferring with the feds, keeping necessary statistics and information, writing reports, and applying for the grants.

Some local development agencies measure their success by the amount of federal dollars they obtain. That's not a bad yardstick.

But concentration on grants may distort your analysis of what your community really needs. You may be letting the kinds of grants available lead you when you should be objectively deciding what program or projects will strengthen your community most. Moreover, sooner or later the grants expire and you are left with a staff which must be paid from city revenues. What do you do then?

Organize an ombudsman program

An ombudsman program is the one-stop city hall office where the businessman can get answers to problems connected with some city activity or regulation. The development office is the logical place for the ombudsman function. It acts as the businessman's voice in city hall.

To most businessmen, city hall is uncharted territory. They are a little bit awed by the elected officials. They don't know where to go or to whom to relate their corporate problems. They may wander from office to office, may be given erroneous information, may have to wait considerable periods of time, may be dealt with curtly or coldly. The result is often a frustrated, disgruntled businessman who later describes to his friends the many lazy, discourteous, stupid public servants wasting taxpayers' money. "No wonder my taxes are so high" is a common expression of dissatisfaction.

Since it no longer is disputed that the most important activity of an urban economic development department is retaining the city's present businesses, keeping these businessmen happy and contented is extremely important. It's also recognized that an essential plant location factor these days is a friendly city administration. The ombudsman activity relates to both keeping the business executive happy and convincing him that the city administration is friendly toward business. It helps broaden the development contacts among businesses and helps keep businesses in the city.

Strengthen city hall support

Without strong support—active support—from the mayor, a development department is severely handicapped. The mayor must show by attitude, talk, and action that he believes in economic development. This stance is much more prevalent today than a few years ago.

Strong support connotes recommending an adequate budget to enable the department to do the job, and exercising patience about results. Development often is a long-term activity, particularly for a new department, or if the economy is in a tailspin. You can't see immediate results like you can from filling potholes. But economic development is now recognized as one of the most important functions in a city. Most city departments are rated by how much they spend; the economic development department is the only one rated

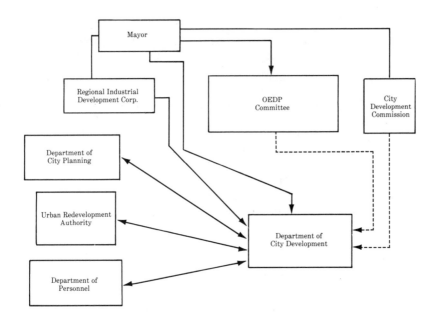

Figure 2. Pittsburgh city development inter-agency chart.

by the increased revenue it generates through creating more jobs and increasing the tax ratables (from new and expanded plants).

Strong support from the city council is also required. The members of the council are well-known in the city, particularly in the areas in which they live. With their contacts and knowledge, they can be of invaluable assistance to the development department. To obtain and keep their cooperation, they should be kept informed of the plans, programs and activities of the department. This cannot always be done at council meetings which are public, since much of the work of the development department is conducted on a confidential basis. It may be necessary to work on an individual basis with these persons.

The importance of working closely and in harmony with other city departments, particularly planning and urban development, has already been mentioned. The personnel department is also important since it handles training programs and is involved with labor management. Figure 2 shows graphically the relationship between the development department and other agencies.

Summary

In summary, some of the activities which a development office might want to incorporate or include in its program are:

1. Organize and set goals.
2. Develop basic economic data.
3. Obtain visibility and cooperation.
4. Establish land banks.
5. Know your financing capabilities.
6. Consider building rehabilitation.
7. Develop minority entrepreneurs and jobs.
8. Obtain federal grants.
9. Organize an ombudsman program.
10. Strengthen city hall support.

PART 3

Public Sector Intervention in the Marketplace

Leveraging: The Patchwork Quilt Approach to Development

Kenneth P. Fain

Small communities throughout the country are highly diverse in size, history, population, economic base or potential. But in varying degrees, all face the same fundamental economic development problem: How to foster economic growth, revitalization and new employment opportunities with limited public resources.

Put another way, how can towns help facilitate business expansion, new business development or downtown revitalization when funding sources for even basic services are at a premium?

The answer is surprisingly easy to state: leverage private investment and financing with public capital. At its core, leveraging is simply a process of attracting additional funds for a program or project by making an initial investment.

Though easily said (and said often these days by federal and state officials) prescriptions that "ye shall leverage" are not so readily understood or carried out, especially in towns having little experience in committing public funds to stimulate private investment. In many such towns, neither town officials, the local business community nor local financial institutions have clear-cut notions about the need for leveraging, its many benefits or how best to go about doing it.

Matching grants, familiar to most town and township officials, represent one obvious form of leveraging, though strictly from public sources. Two or more funding sources are combined to help do a job for which one source would be insufficient.

Reprinted with permission from *National Community Reporter*, published by the National Association of Towns and Townships, March 1984. More information is available from NATaT, 1522 K Street, N.W., Suite 730, Washington, D.C. 20005, (202) 737-5200.

In economic-development finance, the principle of leveraging prevails and local government's role is precisely the same as it is in matching grants. Through provision of a limited amount of public funds, the business development or downtown revitalization program stimulates private investment, both debt and equity. That private investment, in turn, helps create employment opportunities, tax base and economic vitality.

Indirect leveraging

There is nothing mysterious about the concept of leveraging for economic development. In fact, most towns probably use one form of indirect leveraging for economic development, regularly. Every time a sewer line is constructed, a road is built, or a bridge goes up, there is an incentive for the private sector to take advantage of these facilities. When businesses take advantage of public facilities to expand operations or hire more employees, indirect leveraging for economic development is at work.

All of these publicly funded activities stimulate or induce the investment of private capital, often in amounts far in excess of the public funds spent. Houses are built and purchased, businesses expand or locate, jobs are created—because the town chose to make an investment of its own.

Indirect leveraging for economic development is most effective when it is planned and when the public expenditures are phased to provide orderly development based on overt economic objectives and targeted benefits, such as in industrial park development. That's a tall order, even for the most sophisticated or largest local governments. But even if it were standard operating procedure in small communities to leverage funds for economic development, it would still be only "indirect" leveraging at its best.

For most communities, the strategies and techniques of indirect leveraging may need further refinement, but the concept of stimulating private investment through the provision of public facilities, improvements or tax benefits is well known and accepted. It is part of the traditional approach to economic development, one that demonstrates a "good fit" with the expected and accepted functions of local government.

Passive approach is no longer enough

Indirect leveraging is, however, a generally passive approach and does not usually involve the township in what may be the most critical part of the business decision-making process: matching affordable financing to business plans.

Though there are times when business expansion or location decisions are contingent on provision of certain public improvements or tax breaks, even the most aggressive use of these inducements may not be enough. If the businesses involved cannot obtain sufficient financing under acceptable terms and conditions, no expansion, construction or business start-up will occur.

Similarly, if main street merchants cannot afford the cost of financing storefront facade improvements, upgrading and expanding inventory, and additional advertising, then the benefits of those expensive street, curb and gutter improvements, tree plantings, etc., may not be so self-evident.

Community preparedness programs, good planning and provision of public facilities are important and should not be avoided. But to make things happen in local economic development in the 1980s, local officials can and must reorient themselves and develop additional approaches to using public funds. Officials must become part of the business development, deal-making process through direct participation in business financing.

Direct leveraging

Use of public funds to provide additional capital, lower-cost debt financing or guarantees for debt financing is often called direct leveraging. Direct leveraging may not be a role with which town or township officials are comfortable or familiar. Nevertheless, it is a role that is increasingly necessary to help foster economic development and revitalization.

A township's willingness to use direct leveraging to facilitate business development and revitalization provides many benefits—some immediate, others over longer periods of time.

Probably the most important of these benefits is that direct leveraging allows the town to help shape its own economic destiny rather than passively waiting for the uncertainty of market forces to mystically implement the town's economic development plans. Other key advantages and benefits of using public funds (which include federal or state grants, tax revenues and local dollars) as part of the package of business financing include:

Flexibility Direct leveraging is potentially, by definition, the most flexible economic-development tool town officials have at their disposal. Public funds can be used to help tailor special investment and loan programs that fit the specific and immediate needs of the town, businesspeople and lenders. Public funds can be used to reduce interest rates, extend terms (repayment schedules), increase capital investment (downpayment amounts) or do any combination of these activities to assist business.

Maximum return on investment Direct leveraging almost always provides the most benefits for the least expenditure of public funds.

A $100,000 Community Development Block Grant (CDBG) could be used to provide ten $10,000 grants for storefront rehabilitation. The work might be done, ten properties might be improved, but the businesses might have no more customers than before. More importantly, the $100,000 will have virtually disappeared, from the town's perspective, except perhaps for some minor increases in property tax assessments.

On the other hand, that same $100,000 could be used to create a $400–$500,000 below-market-rate loan pool that would facilitate storefront rehabilitation and provide working capital to help 30 to 50 businesses expand, add new lines of merchandise or services and construct buildings. In addition, the funds used to support the pool can, as loans are paid down or paid off, be returned to the town for other economic development activities.

Federal and state funds are precious commodities: to pass those funds through in the form of grants for private use may be easy but it's extremely wasteful, especially when direct leveraging opportunities are available.

Funds retention/recycling   Many of the best direct-leveraging programs feature uses of public funds that eventually enable the town to recoup all or part of its investment. Loan repayments, the sale of rehabilitated buildings and the sale or lease of industrial shell buildings are examples of actions that can result in return of the town's CDBG or Urban Development Action Grant (UDAG) funds for reuse in other economic-development activities.

Timeliness   A low-cost loan program can be planned and operational in much less time than can public facilities projects which might not produce much private investment. In fact, once lenders understand the town's objectives, they can help set up such a program in a matter of weeks, if necessary. Also, some state and federal programs are moving toward multiple funding cycles. Many states administering CDBG programs have established quarterly application and funding cycles for economic-development projects.

Increased community confidence   Direct-leveraging agreements with local lenders serve as evidence that the town is not standing still, is willing to work with the business community in an active partnership and has experts in finance committed to the town's future.

Enhanced grantsmanship capacity   Competition for many grants has increased dramatically without any corresponding increase in the total grants authorized. Consequently, federal and state grant programs are increasingly emphasizing leveraging and private sector participation. In reviewing grant applications, federal and state officials continue to add weight to leveraging private resources as a factor in determining grant awards.

Advantages of leveraging for the lender

Financial institutions in small communities are very much "anchored" businesses. They are tied to their communities and local market areas by their charters and often by state law that specifies how and where they can conduct business. Consequently, for most smaller banks and savings associations, the social, physical and economic health of the communities they serve directly affects their own fortunes. When a local economy is stagnating or in severe decline, deposits flow out of the institution and loan demand is low. Hence the profit potential for the financial institution is, in a very real sense, tied to the potential for growth in the community.

Although this general consideration can provide powerful incentives for community banks to participate in public-private leveraging programs, there are several other major benefits local lenders could enjoy:

Enhanced image in the community   Participation in local, economic-development programs helps local financial institutions strengthen their ties to the community and their claims that small banks know and serve their customers best. This is no small accomplishment given the fact that small financial institutions are being threatened by competition from large banks and S&Ls from out of town and even out of state.

Opportunity to expand customer base   Through provision of subsidized, low-interest-rate loans, use of loan guarantees or other leveraging tools, lenders can provide financing to customers who might not have qualified under normal credit standards or who simply could not have afforded financing at market rates. In essence, these loans would not have been made and a potential customer that might have become a loyal, longstanding one, would be lost. Leveraging programs allow the lender to expand the market.

Immediate income generation   Putting leveraged loans on the books, especially when economic conditions may have kept loan demand low, makes money for the financial institution. Usually, the lender obtains a market rate for his or her part of the loan; the subsidy is provided by using public funds.

Secondly, lenders also receive loan origination fees and servicing fees. If participation in public-private financing programs was not profitable, few financial institutions would even consider it.

Both small communities and their small financial institutions can benefit tremendously by combining resources in public-private partnerships for economic development. To develop that partnership, however, towns and townships must be willing to commit public funds for use in direct leveraging. They must become a direct party to the business financing process.

Assessing Public Incentives for Private Development

Stephen B. Friedman

In the past few years, the role of local governments in urban revitalization projects has changed. Many local governments have become
involved in helping to finance, provide public improvements, and
otherwise aid such downtown revitalization projects as hotels, office buildings, and retail malls.

Increasingly, local governments have been using essentially local powers to aid these projects, whether or not federal funds are
involved. Tax increment financing, tax abatement, and industrial
revenue bonds (IRBs) for commercial projects have become common.

Local governments and developers are becoming aware of just
what can be done to make revitalization feasible. The federal government role is shifting. Enterprise zones require local government
decisions on what areas can, in fact, prosper with the incentives offered. In addition, with continued high interest rates, the 1981 Economic Recovery Tax Act, and changes in private sector development
finance, local governments will be faced more and more with new
issues about how to use revitalization incentives. These will not be
easy questions for local government.

Virtually all incentives involve a real local government stake:
direct expenditures and obligations (even if underwritten by expected tax increment revenues), forgone tax revenues, or possible
implications of an industrial revenue bond (IRB) default on local
credit ratings (or, at a minimum, as a reflection on local economic
conditions).

Condensed from: Management Information Service Reports, vol. 13, no. 12 (Washington, D.C.: International City Management Association, December 1981). Reprinted
with permission.

Professional managers, with overall responsibility for fiscal restraint, community development, long-term tax base, and economic health, may be facing some unfamiliar decisions. What is a viable revitalization project? How much assistance does it need? What types of assistance will be most effective and cost the local government the least?

These issues affect both large and small communities. The approach to urban rivitalization and development incentives discussed here has been refined through work with such cities as Appleton, Wisconsin; Des Moines, Iowa; Charlotte, North Carolina; Cincinnati, Ohio; Rochester, New York; and South Haven, Michigan.

This article is a brief introduction to analyzing development projects and use of incentives available to local government.[1] In general, there are five issues for public officials to address while determining whether or not to provide development incentives:

1. Public revitalization objectives. The projects should contribute to achieving development objectives established by the community. These objectives may include enhancing the local tax base, job development, efficient use of existing public services, and other measurable benefits. Often, less quantifiable objectives are also considered, including historic preservation and other civic concerns. Clear understanding of objectives permits both identification of desired projects and analysis of potential benefits. These benefits serve as the "bottom line" against which the costs of incentives can be checked.

2. Benefits and costs. Public officials should know the benefits of the project and, therefore, what should be the maximum public cost. These benefits may be additions to the tax base, service efficiency, jobs, convenience, or less easily quantifiable benefits such as amenities, or preserved cultural values.

3. Market analysis. Public officials should know whether sufficient market support exists both for projects to be aided and for competing projects in the same area. Public subsidy of, for example, two struggling hotels can and should be avoided. Rehabilitation of an existing building instead of new development may be preferable if vacant older space would otherwise result.

4. Financial feasibility. Public financing tools should improve the financial feasibility of development projects under given market conditions. Financial feasibility analysis can be used to identify the "gap" to be filled by public financial assistance if the project is to be viable. As financing conditions and tax laws have changed, so too has the financial feasibility of projects. The 1981 Economic Recovery Tax Act improves overall return slightly, which can partially offset higher interest rates, for example. With so much change, fi-

nancial analysis for use of incentives is an even more critical element of decision making than in more stable times.
5. Incentive options. Public officials should determine which type of incentive will help the developer the most and cost the city the least.

Public revitalization objectives

There are many approaches to establishing overall objectives for urban revitalization and considering the many public values involved. Many cities have developed plans for downtown areas and other areas that serve as the general basis of revitalization. Planning revitalization includes review and evaluation of a number of factors:

1. Physical conditions in the area
2. Site location, access, surroundings, amenities
3. General market conditions and private sector interests
4. Regulatory constraints
5. Community goals
6. Social, cultural, and amenity values worth preserving
7. Development opportunities and experiences in other cities.

The analysis of these conditions and opportunities will provide a context of realistic development objectives for a community. Each proposed project can then be evaluated in terms of how well it contributes to meeting the objectives involved. Is the proposed project what the community wants and needs to achieve revitalization of the area where it is undertaken?

Benefits and costs

A broad sense of the desirability of particular development projects will result from the initial analysis. The next question confronting public officials is: How much is it worth to obtain the project? This analysis should determine how much the project is worth to the public sector, not the private sector. The value to the public sector should be measured first in quantitative terms, because the assistance involved is usually monetary. Several types of benefits can be relatively easily quantified:

1. Net tax contribution (real estate, sales or others)
2. Jobs and indirect taxes
3. Avoided public service costs (for example, from downtown rather than suburban locations, which allows greater use of existing infrastructure)
4. Avoided transit subsidy costs (for example, from downtown rather than suburban locations, where existing routes can carry the load and extensions can be avoided).

Other benefits cannot be easily expressed in dollars but should be considered qualitatively:

1. Convenience and reduced travel for the public
2. Aesthetic benefits
3. Catalytic (i.e., spinoff) potential (and symbolic value).

The benefits may then be used to stimulate other development to determine the public "bottom line," or maximum costs that should be incurred to support the project. Costs include the following:

1. Direct costs of incentives
2. Increases in public service levels and costs (but not costs to repair old infrastructure; those costs would be incurred anyway)
3. Future opportunities preempted.

A project should generate enough public benefits at least to equal the public costs on a time-adjusted basis. Generally, the value of benefits should substantially exceed the costs over the life of the project. The public sector should try to exercise leverage with its resources just as private developers attempt to do with their capital. Only rarely would a project have such symbolic or catalytic value as to warrant use of incentives greater than the value of the quantifiable benefits.

   With the public value of the project understood, the strength of the particular project and its need for assistance can then be evaluated.

Market analysis

Market analysis provides both a broad understanding of the scope of development opportunities in an area and the specific demand, rents, absorption, and occupancy rates for individual development projects. At a given time, there is a finite market for retail, office, hotel, residential, or other land uses in a metropolitan area. Only a share of that market can be captured by any subarea such as downtown. Market conditions may change over time because of growth in regional population, highway access improvements, changing public tastes, and new development forms. A well-prepared market analysis should consider these issues carefully rather than simply projecting past trends, particularly for downtown or other revitalization areas.

   For each category of use, market analysis will determine the gross number of square feet supportable, attainable rent levels, and detailed uses such as specialty retail, class of office buildings, and other factors. The market analysis should include both quantitative and qualitative evaluation of overall population and income, access, aesthetics, amenities, and what people want based on both behavior and survey research. Existing facilities and competitive conditions should be reviewed. Gaps, weaknesses, and opportunities should be identified.

Some projects that will appear highly desirable for social, aesthetic, or other reasons may not be fully supported by the market. The issues that the market analysis can help resolve include basic demand, competition, and impact on occupancy of existing buildings.

In smaller cities, the market for new downtown office space or hotel rooms is often small. Careful consideration of potentially competing projects is therefore important. The office market may be large enough to absorb one new downtown building of 60,000 to 80,000 square feet. Two such buildings would split the market and make both uneconomical. Public officials are faced with a choice, even when using only IRBs. They cannot support both buildings, for if both proceed, both probably will fail.

Similarly, in many communities, there may be insufficient market growth to fill even one new building without adverse effects on occupancy of existing buildings. While public incentives might make the new building feasible, and while the building may improve the image of the area, vacant older space will result. In such situations, support of rehabilitation projects is sensible, but support of net additions of space may not be.

The strength of the market will determine not only the gross number of square feet of space of various types, but also the rent levels, rate of absorption of space, and vacancy. These in turn determine the revenue potential of a project and hence its financial feasibility.

Financial feasibility

Many of the private development projects proposed for urban revitalization are real estate projects to develop office buildings, hotels, apartments, or retail facilities. The uses of public financing and development incentives are related directly to the economics of the particular project, its costs, revenues, and rate of return to investors. Analyzing the financial feasibility of real estate projects is inherently complex. The return on real estate investment is sensitive to interest rates, dependent on the types of depreciation permitted by law and chosen, influenced by the investors' holding expectations, and affected by expectations of future profit at sale. Interest rates and depreciation in particular can dramatically affect the feasibility of a project, as can the terms of joint venture agreements. This section will briefly discuss four key issues in determining the financial viability of a real estate development project:

1. Sources of investment return
2. Financing and joint ventures: major changes in the investment context

3. Key measures of financial results
4. What is an acceptable rate of return?

Sources of investment return   Returns to real estate investors
come from three sources. First is the cash flow from the property
after expenses and debt service are paid. The higher the rents and
lower the expenses and debt service, the greater the cash flow.

The second source of return is tax benefit. Real estate is one of
the few investments not subject to the "at-risk" provisions of the
tax code that limit losses to the amount invested. As a result, losses
attributable to depreciation or interest expense (subject to investment income expense limitation) can offset or shelter income from
other sources. The 1981 Economic Recovery Tax Act has dramatically changed depreciation provisions by establishing an Accelerated Cost Recovery System (ACRS). "Useful lives" have been replaced by shorter periods, with most real estate investments to be
depreciated over 15 years, compared with periods of up to 40 years
under the old law. This has the effect of improving returns on investment slightly, other factors being equal.

The 1981 tax act also provides tax credits for substantial rehabilitation of buildings over 30 years old or which are historic
structures (on the National Register of Historic Places or in an historic district). Buildings 30 years old are eligible for a tax credit of
15 percent of rehabilitation costs; buildings 40 years old are eligible
for a 20 percent credit; and historic structures, a 25 percent credit.
The amount of the credit is deducted from the basis for cost recovery purposes in the 30- and 40-year-old buildings, but not the historic buildings. Substantial rehabilitation is defined as an expenditure equal to the adjusted basis of the property or $5,000, whichever
is *more*. If one assumes that the investor has sufficient tax liabilities, these credits will be a major boost to early years' returns. Most
important, these 1981 tax act provisions change the relative position
of rehabilitation projects by increasing return from such projects
more than the return is increased in new projects. The 1981 tax act
provisions otherwise simply improve equally the return from all
other real estate investments.

The third source of return is proceeds from sale of the property.
The proceeds include any gain in value over time. The capital gain at
sale (both increase in price and the amount of depreciation taken) is
partly or wholly taxed at an effective maximum rate of 20 percent.
This compares with a top ordinary income tax rate of 50 percent
under the new law. If an accelerated form of depreciation or the Special Accelerated Cost Recovery tables were used, a portion of the
gain may be subject to recapture (determined by the difference between depreciation—not original—value and sale price) and taxed
as ordinary income. If straight-line depreciation was used (old useful lives or the new 15-year term), recapture would not apply.

Real estate projects traditionally have also been used for leverage. The owner's equity would be only a portion of total project cost, with the rest borrowed. Typically, borrowing resulted in positive leverage (i.e., a greater total return on investment). With high interest rates, borrowing can create negative leverage (i.e., it reduces total return on investment).

Investors in real estate projects use the three sources of return along with leverage and different financing vehicles to optimize their returns given the capital available to them, as well as what they determine as their investment objectives (short-term or long-term; income or tax shelter; low risk or high yields).

Financing and joint ventures: major changes in the investment context   The major sources of mortgage funds for commercial and multifamily residential real estate traditionally have been life insurance companies and mortgage banking firms. A fixed-rate, long-term mortgage is provided based on the project's net operating income. After a project is up and operating, a pension fund, or more recently a foreign investor, might purchase a building outright. Today, in response to inflation in prices and continued high interest rates, many traditional lenders want to be at least part owners. At a minimum, they want to participate in growth in rental income. As a result, many developers now find that lenders may want a 50 percent equity position in exchange for financing. Alternatively, lenders may make a loan but require a rental growth or sales price "kicker" (a percentage of the sale profits) to protect them from inflation. Pension funds and limited partnerships are playing growing roles in equity funding. The key to a project in many cases has become not market, site, or zoning, but instead the ability to arrange some form of financing.

Some observers think that as (or if) interest rates seem to be peaking, lenders will seek to lock in high rates and some straight mortgages may return. Even so, it seems likely that lenders will continue to hedge their positions to protect against inflation. For the foreseeable future, financing terms are likely to vary from project to project. This will make the public official's job more difficult since the terms of private sector financing will vary with each prospective financing service.

Key measures of financial results   The overall return on investment, cash flow, and equity requirements can be influenced by the public incentives available. The public official needs to determine how close the project is to being a competitive investment, and where the project requires assistance. Conversely, it is important to determine the viability of a project in order to decide if a developer *does not* need incentive assistance. To do this, the financial analyst must evaluate the following aspects of the project's financial picture.

Net operating income (NOI)   This is the income before debt service but after all operating expenses are paid. It determines the amount of debt service that can be covered. Lenders usually require the NOI to be 1.25 to 1.35 times the debt service to allow for error in projecting revenues and the risk associated with a particular project. Risk will reflect both the market and the type of project.

Cash flow   A positive cash flow after debt service is (usually) required, although many projects can be expected to absorb negative cash flow in the first two or three years.

Equity requirements   Required equity is the difference between total project costs and the amount of debt that can be covered by net operating income.

Return on investment   The overall return can be calculated on a discounted cash flow basis. This includes the expected future income from the project, tax shelter benefits, and, in most cases, assumed profits from disposition. (Discounting adjusts for the fact that money to be received in the future is worth less than funds in hand today. Discounting reduces such returns to their present worth. The desired rate of return can be selected as the discount rate, and if the sum of the present values exceeds the initial investment, that return has been achieved.)[2] Present value[3] calculated with a predetermined discount rate can be used. Alternatively, the internal rate of return (IRR) can be determined. The IRR is the same as the discount rate that would result in a present value of 1.00 for a particular project.

Although these four aspects of the project's financial picture provide a reasonable basis for evaluating the need for the incentives, other measures may also be used in particular cases. The information for further analysis often can be obtained from the developer's *pro formas* (projections of anticipated income expenses, cash flow, and depreciation). Since the developer presumably wants assistance, it is not unreasonable to require this information. Otherwise, the city will have to develop its own *pro forma* for the project. This analysis will permit public officials to determine the type and amount of incentive needed.

The public sector must then identify the incentive options that most effectively address the particular problems of the project under review and determine which has the greatest effect at the lowest cost to the community. This requires testing various options and estimating the impacts on operating costs, income, equity needs, and returns. Different problems require different solutions, as is discussed in a later section.

What is an acceptable return?   Many factors affect real estate investors' expected returns on investment. It is important that public officials realize that incentive decisions are made in that context.

Expected returns are influenced by competition for investors' funds. Today's widespread availability of money market funds is symbolic of both the competition and the inflation which dominate the investment climate. Even the small investor now has expectations for high short-term investment results. An additional factor in determining what is a reasonable return is the tax situation. Since a large proportion of return from real estate investment can come from tax shelters, after-tax returns are often measured. Most competing investments usually are reported on a pretax basis. The investor's tax status also varies. Almost all income of pension funds is tax exempt. Life insurance companies are taxed at a lower effective top rate than are other corporations or individuals.

On balance, after-tax internal rates of returns in the upper teens were likely to have been competitive in late 1981. In many communities, however, there are also investors who will accept lower rates of return from an important civic project. Hence this "patient" money can often be had with the promise of only a lower return.

Professional expertise should be sought in determining competitive return rates. Help is available from real estate industry, banking, accounting, and other financial industry sources.

Incentive options

Local development incentives can help address three financial problems:

1. Insufficient net operating income (to cover debt service and achieve a positive cash flow)
2. Shortage of equity capital (to reach the necessary debt to equity relationship possible with projected income and expenses)
3. Insufficient return on investment (to be competitive with alternative investments).

The financing tools and the 1981 tax act's cost recovery and investment tax credit provisions each work at the margin to improve returns or otherwise enhance viability of a project (e.g., reduce equity requirements). Increases in financing costs marginally reduce the viability of projects with each rise in interest rates because debt service may exceed acceptable debt coverage ratios with traditional equity requirements and attainable rents. As interest rates drop and alternative equity structures are developed, some projects that would have required assistance in the past will become viable. Others will be brought to the margin of viability and to the point where public incentive tools can be of use.

Different financial tools are effective with different problems, and the cost to the public sector varies significantly depending on which tool is used, and how. This is discussed generally below.

Insufficient net operating income   Insufficient net operating income can be addressed in several different ways. Without public aid, the developer would generally increase equity, if available, in order to close the gap, or reduce the size of the project. Since capital is short, and since increasing equity reduces return on investment, other alternatives are attractive. These alternatives are:

Option 1: IRBs   The first alternative is to reduce the costs of debt service through IRBs if the project qualifies. This option has no direct cost to the city and may improve the developer's cash position dramatically.

Option 2: Improve the rental income from the building   This may be done in a soft market by a long-term lease of space for a public agency.

Option 3: Reduce borrowing needs   Reduce the developer's total borrowing needs by reducing development costs, for example, by land write down, or by the provision of public parking.

Option 4: Tax abatement   This is the most expensive option. It may be particularly useful if the developer projects a problem only in the early years, so that the exemption can be limited to three years or some other short term. (Income-based assessment in the early years may in part accomplish the same thing.)

These options will improve the developer's cash position. Once a positive cash flow is attained for a given project, tax abatement is of limited further use because it is taxable as income and counters the tax shelter benefits of depreciation. IRBs may still be of further use because, while they have the same effect on taxable income, they are applied to the entire "leveraged" mortgage amount and, hence, increase return on investment fairly effectively.

Shortage of equity   Developers, particularly local ones, may have only a certain amount of capital of their own or available through investment syndicates to invest in a project. As interest rates have climbed, developers have been forced to increase equity to keep debt service within operating income or to exchange an equity position for favorable debt terms. The options for this problem are related to reducing capital costs or reducing interest rates to close the gap between the available capital and the maximum loan the operating income will support.

The increased problems with equity are leading to a great deal of change in how projects are structured financially. Joint ventures are becoming commonplace, with equity capital from pension funds, insurance companies, and limited partnerships. The limited partnership is a particularly attractive vehicle, because it allows full use of tax benefits which, as noted, contribute a major share of the return on investment. This results from each partner using tax losses to shelter their incomes, commonly in the 50 percent marginal tax bracket even under the new tax law. Public officials should expect to see proposed projects that include fairly complex equity structures. While raising equity is principally a private sector responsibility, the public sector can assist with a number of measures that reduce required capital or extend debt coverage of the building's income. Alternatives for doing this include:

Option 1: IRBs   IRBs can permit the same operating income to cover a larger debt because of lowered interest rates. Required debt service ratios will not be affected, however.

Option 2: Land cost write down (also parking)   Using tax increment financing or other sources, the public sector can provide land at reduced cost or virtually free. This reduces total capital costs but allows the developer to include the land value for mortgage purposes. The same logic applies to any parking or other capital facilities the developer might have to provide. Unless it is owned by the developers, parking will not increase mortgage value or provide increased leverage.

Option 3: Second mortgage   By using TIF or other capital sources, the public sector can provide a second mortgage (with appropriate right to cure any default and prevent foreclosure). This reduces equity needs and may increase return on investment since the investment is lower. Payments will affect cash flow, but payment may be linked to future sale or to gains in cash flow.

Option 4: Leases   In leasing alternatives, the public sector (using TIF, UDAG, or other funds) purchases the land or other elements of the capital costs and leases them back to the developer. A subordinated lease on the land (the lease obligation takes second place to the mortgage) allows the capitalized value of the leasehold on the land to be included in determining the size of the mortgage and hence increases leverage. Such a lease also permits the entire cost to be deducted as an expense. If the land were owned, it could not be depreciated and only interest would be deductible.

Option 5: Direct equity positions   In the late 1970s, a number of cities discussed direct public provision of equity capital. In exchange, the city would take an ownership share and participate in profits, but it would also share the risk. Capital sources discussed included Urban Development Action Grants, bond proceeds, local development corporations subscribed to by local businesses, stock sales, or prospectively, other public program funds. In fact, few such uses of public funds have actually occurred and been recorded. Nevertheless, UDAG projects come close to a means of providing equity or at least substituting for it. UDAG grants have been used as mortgage loans with low interest or interest deferred until later years of a project. The community did not necessarily receive an ownership position. In addition to the source of funds, true equity joint ventures between public and private sectors are also likely to have problems arising from the different objectives and decision making requirements of the two parties.

Insufficient return on investment   Return on investment can be enhanced by all of the techniques listed above except by direct equity participation. With direct public equity, the public sector would generally take its proportionate share of the return; hence, the developer's return would be unaffected.

Different methods of increasing return on investment have varying levels of efficiency in terms of public cost compared with private effectiveness. Increasing borrowed capital and reducing equity without reducing cash flow, such as through land write down, is very effective. If there is sufficient cash flow to pay leasing costs, the subordinated lease is even more effective. Tax exemption is extremely inefficient, since it is taxable to the developer and therefore reduces tax shelter benefits. Each dollar of tax abatement increases return by only 50 cents.

Evaluating the options   The options available to most communities include capital expenditures for parking or land write down; lowered interest rates through IRBs; tax exemption; second mortgage; leases, including subordinated leases; public agency anchor tenancy; and, perhaps in the future, an equity position. Each of these options has different costs and risks to the public sector and different effectiveness potential for private development projects.

Formal cost-effectiveness analysis on a discounted basis reflecting the cost of public borrowing is recommended as the way to determine which option to use. This approach is described in *How to Attract Private Investments into the Inner City through Use of Development Subsidies* by Gary N. Conley.[4] An alternative to discounted analysis over the life of the incentive is to estimate and compare the average annual cost of alternative incentives to the public sector.

In one such analysis, Conley concludes that the subordinated lease had the greatest cost effectiveness, followed by second mortgages and land cost write downs. (However, this can vary substantially.) These incentives address squarely a problem of lack of equity capital, but may not address as effectively a relatively weak market, thereby resulting in difficulty with debt service or such other cash expenditures as taxes. This can be a problem, particularly in the early years of a project. Conley's finding emphasized the impact of discounted return on investment—a key measure—but did not look at such other problems as cash available for operations or the major impact of sale proceeds on the return. Often, cash availability is a major problem in early years of a project. Therefore, IRBs coupled with a short-term tax abatement (or assuring that the assessor uses actual building income for early years' assessments) may be required. High interest rates have virtually required greater equity for a project to be financially viable as well. If equity is limited, for example, with a well-intentioned but small local developer, it may be critical to be able to afford more debt service through increasing net operating income.

Conclusion

Local governments can assure that limited funds for development incentives are used most effectively through careful analysis of specific projects, including their desirability and their need for financial assistance. This process can be complex and may require outside assistance with financial and cost effectiveness analysis. Only by performing such analysis can a public official knowledgeably negotiate the use of public development incentives to induce private projects that otherwise would not occur. Without such analysis, incentives may be used too liberally, too sparingly, or otherwise inappropriately.

1. A portion of this report was originally prepared as Chapter 7, "Using Incentives: Guidelines for Project Review and Analysis," in *Iowa's Community Development Incentives: An Evaluation.* That report was prepared by the author while previously employed at Real Estate Research Corporation under contract to the Iowa Office for Planning and Programming. Their permission to use that material is gratefully acknowledged. At the same time that the Iowa project was being conducted, the author participated in the development of *Economics of Revitalization: A Decisionmaking Guide for Local Officials* prepared for the Heritage Conservation and Recreation Service of the U.S. Department of the Interior. That project was directed by Margery al Chalabi and managed by Robert Miller. Their willingness to share ideas between the two projects and for this paper are gratefully acknowledged.

2. Greer, Gaylon E. *The Real Estate Investment Decision.* Lexington Books, Lexington, Massachusetts, 1979. See particularly chapters 7, 8, and 9 on measures of investment worth.

3. For a discussion of the concept of present value, see Chapter 19, "Capital Budgeting," in *Management Policies in Local Government Finance.* International City Management Association, Washington, D.C., J. Richard Aronson and Eli Schwartz, eds., 1981. See also chapters 7, 8, and 9 of *The Real Estate Investment Decision,* by Gaylon Greer (see note 2).

4. Conley, Gary N. *How to Attract Private Investments into the Inner City through Use of Development Subsidies.* National Council for Urban Economic Development, 1730 K Street, N.W., Washington, D.C. 20006, no date.

Shifting Factors in Plant Location

— Robert M. Ady

In this article, I will attempt to develop a clear and concise statement of what has been happening regarding the relative importance of facility location factors and what is likely to happen in the future. My observations are based on the experiences of the Fantus Company in advising industries on where they should build facilities.

Before I discuss this topic, it might be well to take a few minutes to define terms. First, the factors affecting facility location are typically divided into two rather distinct groups: (1) cost factors, those which can be conveniently measured in terms of dollars and cents, and (2) noncost factors, those which cannot be measured directly or conveniently in terms of dollars and cents and yet must be carefully examined during the site selection process to insure the success of the proposed facility.

There are five broad categories which represent about 90 percent of the total geographically variable cost factors associated with a typical plant location study. These are: labor costs, transportation costs, utility costs, occupancy costs (or financing costs) and tax costs. These costs are usually treated as recurring costs and therefore annualized, and their totals represent a major input into locational decisions by most companies.

In terms of noncost, or subjective, factors there are usually a myriad of criteria investigated during the course of a facility location project. The list may be as short as a half-dozen or as long as 100 or more. However, most company lists include at least: labor availability, labor attitudes, electric power and natural gas reliability and dependability, site suitability and living conditions.

Reprinted from *Industrial Development*, November/December 1981, by permission of the publisher, Conway Data, Inc., Atlanta, Ga. No further reproduction is permitted. The original includes figures and tables that further illustrate the text.

In order to analyze shifts that we see occurring in facility location, I will discuss cost factor changes and key noncost factor changes separately.

Past cost factor trends

Let us consider cost factor changes first. Transportation costs and financing costs have increased much more dramatically during the past 10 years than the cost of labor, electric power or local property taxes. An examination of the reasons for the different rates of increase among these factors will help determine what has happened and what is likely to happen in the future.

Labor   Labor cost will no longer play as important a role in the site selection process as it did during the 1960s and early 1970s. This is true for a number of reasons.

First, legislative increases in the minimum wage have flattened regional differentials being paid to unskilled workers and compacted company wage scales.

Second, future shortages for most skilled labor will place companies in national competition for these workers.

Third, regional pockets of unskilled labor tightness will build up rates in selected areas.

Finally, the pressure for plants to continue to operate nonunion will probably result in somewhat more generous wage adjustments in their plants, thereby reducing their hourly advantage versus unionized plants.

During the past 10 years, hourly wage costs have about doubled, not too much different from the rate of inflation. We expect the same to hold true for the 1980s, with wage costs doing no better than keeping pace with inflation.

Transportation   Changes in transportation costs during the past 10 years have been startling. Indeed, increases have occurred with such rapidity that tariff publishing agencies may now be making more money than the carriers that they serve.

Between 1970 and 1980 common motor carrier class rates in central states were subjected to 26 general increases. The Class 100 rate on shipments under 1,000 pounds for distances of 200 miles increased from $3.51 per hundredweight as of January 1, 1970, to $11.33 after the 26th increase granted October 1, 1980, a 10-year jump of 223 percent.

Similarly, private trucking costs have doubled during the past five years from about $0.60 per mile to $1.20 per mile. Rail rates have shown an even more dramatic increase. In the East a $1.00 per hundredweight rate in 1970 has been increased 23 times and nearly fourfold to a rate of $3.71 today. Similar increases have occurred in Southern and Western regions.

What this means is that the fuel crisis, coupled with labor rate and investment increases, has fallen heavily upon shipping costs and that strategic market and raw material orientation has gained significantly in importance to the industrial site seeker.

As a natural by-product of deregulation, more and more firms have moved, and will move, into private and contract motor carriage. Since regulated motor carrier rates in the South have historically been 25 percent or more below similar mile-for-mile rates within the North, this advantage for the South will erode.

Even though the Fantus Co. expects the rate of increase in transportation cost to slow somewhat during the next 10 years, its rate of increase will still be faster than inflation. And its importance as a cost factor will increase vis-a-vis the other factors.

Energy The scenario is different for electric power cost. We feel that these costs, which have escalated very rapidly during past years, will continue on a fast track for the next 10 years.

New, potentially less costly sources of generating capacity will not be available until the latter part of this time frame. Costs and environmental problems associated with nuclear energy will continue to plague the development of this energy source in the near term. Our best guess is that the over 200 percent increase in industrial power costs felt during the 1970s will be duplicated during the 1980s.

Taxes Probably one of the best bargains for the industrial site seeker in the U.S. at the present time is the level of personal property tax levied against the corporation. As competition among the states for new facilities has increased during the past few years, more and more states have sought to improve their business climates to attract new industries. Although median effective tax rates have increased from about 2 percent to 4 percent of total investment during the past 10 years, more states are granting full or partial exemption to various classes of property. For example, during the past five years, the number of states granting full or partial exemption from ad valorem taxes on production machinery has jumped from 9 to 16, while the number of states granting full or partial exemption on manufacturers' inventories has increased from 18 to 35.

Similarly, state levies on corporate income have remained relatively stable. Indeed, during the past five years only two states have had increases in these rates, and in both cases the increases were minor.

It is difficult to evaluate whether or not Reagan economics vis-a-vis increased pressure for additional manufacturing jobs will result in significantly heavier or lighter tax levies against business. Our best guess is that state tax levies against business will increase much faster during the next decade as states and cities will be required to fund a greater proportion of various social programs currently funded at the federal level. Once a few states break the present rigidity in corporate tax levies, our guess is that the dam will burst and rates nationally will take a quantum leap similar to what happened in the early 1970s.

Occupancy costs   The last cost item, occupancy, has risen faster than any other during the 1970s. Both key elements that make up this cost, construction and interest rates, have doubled during the past 10 years. A $2 million building in 1970 cost $4,444,000 in 1980. A typical revenue bond interest rate in 1970 of 7 percent nearly doubled to 13 percent by 1980 and stands even higher now. Therefore, the annual cost to amortize a 25-year loan on a similar sized facility in 1970 and 1980 jumped from $169,800 to $601,717, an increase of over 250 percent.

We see some leveling of this factor in the future, with construction costs not increasing as rapidly and interest rates stabilizing in the 10 to 15 percent range.

Future cost factor trends

Now that each of the cost factors has been discussed individually, we can summarize how their relative importance has changed during the past 10 years and is likely to change during the next 10. Probably the easiest way to analyze these changes is within the context of three identical plants being built at the same location: one in 1970, the next in 1980 and the last in 1990. The identical requirements for these plants are as follows:

Labor: 200 hourly workers

Transportation:

Inbound: 12 million pounds annually Class 35, 500 mile average, by rail.

Outbound: 10 million pounds annually Class 100, 200 mile average, by common motor carrier.

Electric power: 1,000 kw; 2,000 kwh per month

Building investment: 100,000 square feet at $10 per square foot (1970)

Machinery and equipment: $200,000 (1970)

Inventory: $100,000 (1970)

Note the decreasing relative importance of labor from its 60 percent level in 1970 to about 48 percent in 1990. The big gainer is transportation cost, which we project to jump from 35 percent of total operating costs for this plant in 1970 to 44 percent in 1990. Electric power costs will go from 1 to 4 percent, while occupancy costs will hold at 3 percent and local taxes at 1 percent.

Significance of cost vs. noncost factors

Now that expected changes in the five key geographically variable operating costs have been discussed, I must tell you that as a group they have become less important to location decisions in recent years and, in our opinion, they will continue to diminish in importance in future years. Five years ago, we recommended to two-thirds of our clients that they locate in the lowest cost of our finally recommended towns. Now that ratio has dropped to less than half. We foresee this trend continuing as more and more companies become more and more concerned about the living conditions and operating environment in which they are making an investment. Therefore, in addition to forecasting geographically variable costs, the corporate site seeker in the future will have to become much more adept at measuring and evaluating noncost or subjective factors in light of his company policy and/or top management desires.

A cursory review of Fantus client reports during the early 1970s reveals the following key noncost location criteria: unionism, natural gas availability, proximity to interstate highways and proximity to various support services. Another review for 1980 clients showed the following factors overshadowed the previous criteria: environmental concerns, living conditions, service by the newly deregulated industries and electric power availability and reliability.

New concerns

During the next 10 years it is quite probable that new concerns will rise to the fore. Chief among these will be the availability of labor, both skilled and unskilled. Although the present economic downturn has eased immediate manpower pressures, there is every indication that labor shortages will affect most parts of the country during the next 10 years.

It is relatively easy to forecast the working-age population over the next 5 to 10 years, because projections are based on people who have already been born. Today's 10 to 15 year olds will be the 20 to 25 year olds of our population in 10 years, minus an adjustment for those who die in the interim. Based on this simple reasoning, demographers predict a slackening of the working-age population growth rate at least until 1990.

Declining growth rates of the working-age population are echoed in labor force declines. While the labor force grew at a rate of 2.3 percent during the first half of the 1970s, it is expected to grow at a little over 1 percent during the 1980s. Falling growth rates are due to the fact that those born during the post-World War II baby boom have already entered the labor market.

Thus, although the youth labor force numbered 23.7 million in 1977, it is expected to be only 22.4 million in 1990. If it were not for the increased participation of women in the work force, this figure would be even lower.

A lengthy article in the magazine *Small Business Report* demonstrated that national shortages are already evident for industries that need machine operators, mechanics, welders, electricians, draftsmen, tool and die workers, quality control inspectors, mold and pattern makers and pipefitters. It stated that the results of these shortfalls are pronounced. Indeed, regardless of the reasons, the shortage of skilled workers now requires that companies hire 20 percent more employees than were needed 20 years ago to do the same amount of work, resulting in a 20 percent drop in productivity.

Skilled labor shortages are predicted to exacerbate during the 1980s. As robotization takes hold, the most scarce people in the work force will be those who can adjust and maintain $4 and $5 million of automated machinery that must operate round-the-clock to justify its existence.

Colleges continue to falter in their effort to ease the critical shortage that presently exists for programmers. Estimates of jobs available in the computer industry run as high as 54,000 annually, but the nation's colleges will graduate only 11,000 people with bachelor's degrees in this field each year. Strained college budgets and high-paying industrial job offers to capable instructors suggest that this dilemma will continue in the future.

Some states are trying to cope with skilled labor shortages by providing training schools and training subsidies. These states will benefit from much of the industrial growth of the 1980s, but unfortunately if all the existing qualified schools operated 24 hours per day, they still could not fulfill the national demand for skilled workers in the coming decade.

Financial inducements to become more important   The availability of grants, subsidies and inducements will be a major locational criterion during the next 10 years. The sweepstakes for new industry, which has been under way worldwide for a number of years, is about to begin in earnest in the U.S.

As one example, Volkswagen's $102.2 million auto parts manufacturing plant in Barrie, Ontario, will receive a $9.2 million grant for startup costs related to the facility from the Province of Ontario, even though Barrie is not in an economically depressed area. Volkswagen turned down about $100 million in grants that they would have received if they had located in any Canadian area of high unemployment.

The Fujitec Co., Japan's largest independent elevator maker, is building a new $50 million elevator plant in Lebanon, Ohio, for which it has received a $1.85 million direct loan and a $600,000 grant for clearance of the construction site from the state of Ohio.

The competition for new plants among the states and between the U.S. and other industrialized countries will heat up in the future to the resounding advantage of the corporate site seeker. How far it will go will depend on who's in the poker game and how big the pot is, in terms of jobs provided, technology introduced, investment contemplated and prestige of the company.

Water   In addition to continued concern regarding power availability and reliability during the 1980s, another resource will lead in importance among noncost factors. It is water.

Troubles concerning water are already starting to surface. The governors of four Mid-Atlantic states declared water emergencies and established conservation measures which included water restrictions imposed on industry. Long-term water problems in Los Angeles, Denver and suburban Chicago have made national newspapers. Oil shale development and coal gasification in Wyoming could further deplete the water supply of the Upper Colorado Basin and Upper Missouri Basin.

One of our greatest water resources, the Ogallala Aquifer, is predicted to be largely depleted by the year 2000. This aquifer is being lowered one to two feet yearly in some areas. Groundwater is also depleted along the Gulf Coast from Texas through central Louisiana and along the Alabama and Mississippi Gulf.

Industry's use of water will increase from 100 billion gallons per day currently to 312 billion gallons by the year 2000. Improved water management technology will be necessary not only to avoid a national crisis but to allow certain areas to avoid restrictions on new water users, be they industrial, commercial or even residential.

Conclusion
Obviously, the classic and fundamental criteria of plant location will continue to apply during the 1980s. However, few decisions will be made—or will be able to be made—without consideration of the new forces emerging to shape this country's economic geography.

Can Ma and Pa Compete Downtown?

Glen Weisbrod

The past decade has seen continual changes in downtown retail districts. Public and private investments being made to support the stability (if not the growth) of retailing in downtown areas range from new downtown shopping centers and arcades to pedestrian and transit malls. Serious questions still remain, though, concerning just how these projects affect existing downtown business and the extent to which they really help expand the downtown retail market.

The types of businesses located in downtown retail districts are usually very different from those in suburban shopping centers. Shopping centers have a far greater concentration of specialty chain stores than has been common in downtown areas. Thus, a typical downtown retail or service establishment is far more likely to be a small, independent business than its counterpart in a suburban shopping center. These small, independent operations often have deteriorated facilities, are undercapitalized, and now have difficulty obtaining financing for renovation or expansion. In some downtowns, these remaining establishments have stayed in business only by changing their merchandise to serve the lower-income market of inner city neighborhoods. It is because of these conditions that downtown retail establishments are often quite vulnerable to new competition and changed market conditions. This is also why revitalization of downtown business districts is associated with support for small business.

Reprinted with permission from the February 1983 issue of *Urban Land*, published by the Urban Land Institute.

Defining downtown improvements

A program aimed at improving a city's downtown retail district can encompass any of a variety of strategies: sidewalk widenings, amenity improvements, and pedestrian mall projects to improve the physical environment of an existing retail district; public facilities, such as transportation terminals or performing arts centers, intended to help bring added activity to an existing retail district; construction of new shopping facilities (arcades and shopping centers) downtown; central management and promotion for an existing retail district; regulations and subsidies to encourage building improvements; and special tax abatements and subsidies to encourage new entrants. Downtown improvement efforts including one or more of the above elements have been implemented nationwide.

Among the efforts to bolster downtown commercial activity, it is crucial that a distinction be made between those improvements which actually strengthen *existing* retail districts and those which develop a *new* center of commercial activity in the downtown area. The latter may technically be referred to as land redevelopment projects, whereas the former are more accurately revitalization projects. Depending on their location, design, and tenant mix, redevelopment projects can offer competition or support to the existing retail blocks. To a significant extent, the tenant mix of a new downtown shopping center is determined by the developer, in contrast to on-street business districts where tenant mix is largely a product of market forces.

Downtown shopping centers are seen today by developers as a new growth area (especially in metropolitan areas where the suburban market has approached saturation) and by some city officials as a means of improving downtowns. The new shopping facility may be either new construction or a building rehabilitation, and it may be located in the traditional downtown retail district or nearby.

In any case, it is likely to have a substantial impact on the mix of businesses in that area. From the Gallery in Philadelphia to Water Tower Place in Chicago, there are strong economic forces keeping the tenant mix of many of these downtown centers dominated by the same types of major chain stores that typify suburban malls. Wishing to minimize both risk and marketing assistance required by their merchants, mall developers and the financing institutions look to well-known companies with a strong credit rating and proven success at attracting customers—areas in which local entrepreneurs cannot compete. Chain stores are also preferred because of the developer's prior experience working with them in suburban stores. A challenge for new downtown shopping facilities will be to achieve a mix of stores which can help the overall downtown area gain or maintain a reputation for distinctive shopping opportunities not available elsewhere.

Improvements to existing shopping streets

Public programs to support the revitalization of an existing retail district have traditionally concentrated on improvements to upgrade its image and convenience: new pedestrian amenities (e.g., sidewalks, benches, trees, and fountains), improved parking facilities and transit service, the upgrading of street lighting and trash collection, and greater police visibility. The early pedestrian malls of the 1960s relied totally on design improvement as the means of attracting shoppers back to downtown, and some of these projects completely failed to halt the movement of business out of the downtown area. More recent downtown revitalization efforts are incorporating transit malls and auto restricted zones, designed to improve accessibility to downtown business as well as add to the area's physical improvements.

Although initial sales increases from 10 to 30 percent have been claimed for many pedestrian/transit mall projects, studies of downtown business patterns over time have found that the true increases in business growth in the first few years (measured in terms of constant dollars, retail employment, or active retail floor space) more often range from zero to 4 percent annual growth. The success of these projects has varied widely from city to city, with results ranging from significant increases in business growth to continued stagnation and loss of businesses. In general, there is evidence that, at least in the short run, downtown revitalization projects frequently affect business turnover and entry more than they affect total sales volume. But what has been the nature of the changes in those downtowns where major impacts have occurred?

Looking at changes over time in the mix of downtown businesses for various communities with revitalization projects, it is clear that a number of consistent trends do occur. One is a disproportionate increase in new chain stores. In Boston's Downtown Crossing, the new retailers were mostly restaurants and clothing chains. In Philadelphia's Chestnut Street Mall, they were major chains including fast food outlets, stereo shops, and men's clothing. In Chicago's State Street Mall, they were chain stores selling women's sportswear, shoes, and drugs, and in Portland, Oregon, it was fast food and jeans store chains.

One factor common to a number of the downtowns has been the increase in fast-food eating establishments. This results from the fact that there generally has been an increase in pedestrian activity, particularly from lunch-hour patrons working at nearby office buildings. This trend underscores the importance of new office development and its proximity to downtown retail streets.

Where pedestrian activity has increased, the entry of specialty shops, such as moderately priced casual clothing, has often resulted. Such establishments can take advantage of the foot traffic more effectively than, for example, stores selling jewelry, furs, and higher-priced comparison goods, appliances, or other durables. Similarly, a survey of downtown Boston businesses found that among existing merchants, shops selling books, records, and cards—generally "quick stop" types of businesses—had increased sales following completion of the downtown improvement project. Because new sales are concentrated in lower-priced goods and lunches, the overall sales volume may not be as great as the increase in volume of people on the streets.

The opening of downtown performing arts facilities can also have noticeable revitalization impacts. For instance, in both Madison, Wisconsin's State Street and Memphis's Beal Street/Cotton Row the opening of performing arts theaters there led to several new restaurants as well. A survey of businesses entering Boston after it was revitalized confirmed that it was the change in the nature of the market, more than any cosmetic appearance improvements to the area, that influenced their decisions.

The business impacts discussed above can occur, of course, only if the revitalization project is successful in affecting the size and nature of the downtown retail market. Past experience and studies have shown that a large variety of factors work here, including physical design of the project, strength of the local economy, relative importance of the central business district, size and location of the markets of downtown employees and residents, accessibility of the downtown retail blocks to those markets, presence of competing centers, and extent of centralized promotion and management.

Economic incentive policies

Another means of encouraging growth in a downtown business district is the use of tax abatements, subsidized loans, or other economic incentives. Those policies are by and large available only to new entrants into the area and not for existing firms. Given the larger financial and planning resources available to major retail firms, it is not surprising that larger firms and chains are more aware and better able to take advantage of these financial benefits than small firms. At the same time, existing specialty and service merchants can find themselves unable to respond to the newly competitive market through physical renovation, promotion, or a change in product lines, due to their lack of accumulated capital and the difficulty in obtaining loans for working capital. While small firms are not necessarily any more or less preferable than other businesses in a downtown area, it should be recognized that economic incentive programs can affect the types of businesses operating downtown. Cities can discover *post facto* that the effect of short-term tax policies is a major change in an area's character.

Promotion and private investment

Business community involvement in the downtown revitalization projects has varied widely from community to community. A particular benefit of business involvement in the planning and implementation of downtown revitalization projects has been the formation or strengthening of downtown associations which can then play a lead role in the subsequent promotion and sponsorship of activities downtown. Boston's Downtown Crossing Association, Memphis's Center City Commission, the Trenton Commons Commission, and the Central Madison Council are all examples of organizations formed in this way. Similarly, Downtown Denver, Inc., and New Orleans' Downtown Development District are other examples where the downtown organization has subsequently been given additional responsibilities for administering special assessments and ongoing maintenance and development of the revitalization district.

Recognizing the importance of centralized promotional activities to the success of their downtown revitalization projects, a number of local governments have stepped in to get these activities going. In Boston, the city conducted background research and came up with seed money (from a federal grant) to help start the downtown organization. In Madison, Wisconsin, the city has financed a fulltime mall activities coordinator.

Whereas public improvement projects in a number of cities (Memphis, Madison, Trenton) have been supported largely by special assessments paid by area businesses, construction of projects in other cities (Boston, Portland) has been funded entirely by public funds. Even in those downtowns where there are increases in foot traffic and sales as a result of publicly funded improvement projects, the degree of private investment in building renovation and new construction in adjacent areas has, at least in the short run, frequently been disappointingly small. There are examples, however, where substantial building renovation has been concurrent with street improvements, perhaps best illustrated by the new Queen Street Mall in Brisbane, Australia.

A challenge for American downtowns is still to bring in private investment in renovation and construction, coordinated with publicly sponsored improvements to the public spaces. The extent to which these downtown improvement projects affect the size and nature of the downtown retail market should be an important consideration in effective downtown planning.

Revitalizing Downtown Retailing: Trends and Opportunities

Urban Land Institute

This article attempts to summarize some of the basic factors that must be considered by any city attempting downtown retail development. Based on interviews with 40 experts on development and retailing, it describes some of the approaches that are being taken in cities across the country to reverse the declining trends in downtown retail.

Four categories of downtown retail projects are described: downtown shopping malls, specialty or festival retailing, mixed-use projects, and retail street innovations.

It stresses that cities must be realistic in assessing the markets for downtown retail. They are not what they used to be. While each city is unique, four basic submarkets for downtown retail services must be evaluated: close-in households, metropolitan residents, downtown workers, and transient customers such as tourists, conventioneers, and business visitors.

In addition to assessing the mix of customers from these four submarkets which a downtown retail development might attract, a city must take several other factors into account: the extent and location of competing shopping opportunities, the other attractions of downtown that might help attract customers, accessibility and parking convenience, the social character of downtown, the quality

Reprinted with permission of the Urban Land Institute, Washington, D.C. This material was prepared under a contract with the Office of Community Planning and Development, U.S. Department of Housing and Urban Development, April 1983. ULI subsequently published this material in the book *Downtown Retail Development: Conditions for Success and Project Profiles* by J. Thomas Black, Libby Howland, and Stuart L. Rogel with contributions from Ralph R. Widner and Noreen Beiro.

and character of existing downtown retail facilities, and the cost of land and facilities.

Such an assessment can serve as the basis for a realistic downtown retail development strategy. To implement such a strategy, both the public and private sectors in the downtown must be fully committed or most developers will steer clear of getting involved.

Several options exist in carrying out the strategy. A conventional approach can be taken in which public and private interests play traditional roles, or codevelopment involving public and private interests as financial, development, and operating partners is feasible.

Whatever approach is taken, it should be chosen with the eyes of city hall and the civic community wide open to the real possibilities unclouded by nostalgia or unrealistic expectations.

By capitalizing on new opportunities rather than trying to restore the past, cities across the country are beginning to prove that downtown retail can be revitalized.

Reversing the trend: downtown retail revitalization

Throughout the 1950s, 1960s, and 1970s, the retail districts of many cities deteriorated as they lost their formerly dominant role in the metropolitan retail market to suburban shopping.

Yet, despite these trends and in contrast to the 1950s and 1960s, a significant number of cities, working with creative, entrepreneurial developers, have initiated new downtown retail revitalization projects since the early 1970s.

Boston and Baltimore, working with the Rouse Company, have developed the now famous Faneuil Hall/Quincy Market complex and Harborplace. The same developer, in cooperation with the city of Philadelphia, created the Gallery, a 250,000-square-foot, 122-store mall connecting two department stores.

Developer John Portman developed a new 300,000-square-foot retail center as part of a major office, hotel, and retail complex in downtown Atlanta. Urban Investment and Development Corporation developed Water Tower Place in Chicago—a project with 600,000 square feet of retail on seven levels arranged around an atrium.

The list of major downtown retail revitalization projects in small and large cities is impressive: the Crossroads Mall in Bridgeport; the Stamford, Connecticut, Town Center, a 900,000-square-foot regional mall; the Grand Avenue in Milwaukee, a 245,000-square-foot retail project; Town Square in St. Paul, 70 stores in a retail, office, and hotel complex; Louisville Galleria in Louisville, Kentucky; the list goes on. Planning, site acquisition, or construction has begun in cities as diverse as San Diego, St. Louis, Minneapolis, and Charleston, West Virginia.

Four categories of projects   The projects fall into several categories reflecting, in part, the retail market opportunities available to the downtown of each individual city:

1. *Regional shopping malls* downtown that include one or more department stores, are relatively freestanding, and in which retailing is the dominant activity. Such malls are the downtown answer to competition with suburban centers for a share of the metropolitan retail market.
2. *Specialty or festival retailing* containing no large store anchor and concentrating on food, entertainment, specialty, and boutique items in a festival or theme environment designed to attract tourists and conventioneers as well as metropolitan residents.
3. *Mixed-use projects* in which retailing is combined with at least two other components, most often hotel, office, or convention facilities. Mixed-use projects may or may not contain major anchor stores and may also contain specialty or festival characteristics. They are designed to take advantage of a substantial on-site clientele of office workers, hotel guests, or conventioneers as well as to attract metropolitan customers.
4. *Retail street renovations* which are efforts to strengthen and improve an existing storefront retail district by enhancing its attractiveness and accessibility, often by creating a transit or a pedestrian mall.

By no means have all of these efforts proven successful. The financial disappointments with Detroit's Renaissance Center, a 375,000-square-foot mixed-use retail center in a major office and ho-. tel complex, is the best known example. The forces that led to the decline of downtown retailing are powerful and cannot be overcome by wishful thinking or the lack of analysis in advance of undertaking a project of the real market for downtown services.

Since there is a growing interest in and commitment to retail revitalization among developers, city, state and federal governments, civic organizations, and downtown associations, the time is right to assess why some of these downtown projects have succeeded while others have failed.

Differing views on prospects for successful retail development downtown   There is no uniform opinion among the developers and retail trade experts on all of the reasons for success or failure. Conditions vary from city to city and reasons that may be explanatory in one case may not apply in another.

Some experts are bullish. While recognizing the difficulties of pulling off successful projects, they feel that such factors as growing downtown office employment, increased middle- and upper-income interest in close-to-downtown housing in some cities, and tastes for more urbane recreation and tourism all augur well for downtown retail revitalization in selected cities.

Others argue strongly that conventional retailing can only occur downtown in cities where a close-in residential market exists of sufficient scale to support such development. They discount the recent growth in middle- and upper-income households in close-to-downtown areas as insufficient to generate significant buying power or to offset the losses of middle- and upper-income residents suffered by central cities since the 1950s. To make their point, they cite retail successes in Chicago, Stamford, Santa Monica, Glendale, San Francisco, and Manhattan—all cities with strong middle- and upper-income residential populations in and around downtown. To make the other side of their argument, they point to less successful projects in cities such as Detroit, Kansas City, and Springfield, Massachusetts, where there is less close-in buying power.

A third group takes the view that differences between cities are too great to draw general conclusions about what makes for success or failure in downtown retail revitalization.

Realistically assessing the potential market for downtown retail   Even if some retailers and developers are optimistic, some pessimistic, and some noncommittal regarding opportunities for downtown retail revitalization, there is strong agreement on the factors which determine retail investment potential and, therefore, on the factors which must be assessed realistically in evaluating the potential for a major project in a given downtown area. The principal factors stressed by the experts interviewed were:

1.   The size (buying power) of the market that can be attracted to a downtown retail center. Retail projects do not create customers. They must come from somewhere and there are constraints on the drawing power of any retail complex. In fact, that drawing power drops off sharply within 15 to 20 minutes travel time away from the project. Downtown retail projects must combine several different submarkets of customers to generate sufficient sales to make the project feasible. The submarkets include: (a) households living close in for whom the downtown is the most convenient location to shop; (b) the remaining consumers in the metropolitan area who might be attracted downtown occasionally if central city shopping opportunities and attractions outweigh the inconvenience of time and distance; (c) downtown workers; and (d) transients (tourists, business visitors, and conventioneers).

Clearly many factors unique to each city influence the rate at which each individual downtown and retail project can capture a share of each of these four categories of potential customers. However, the size and character of these four submarkets establish the upper limits of retail space that can be supported economically.

A tough-minded, realistic assessment of market potential must evaluate each of these factors. City planning staffs are becoming more knowledgeable about retail markets, so proven, reputable, expert help should be brought in to assess market potential and other factors in advance of undertaking a retail development project. Failure is certain if plans for a project are pinned on hopes or nostalgia rather than hard-headed analysis.

2. The extent, location, and character of competing shopping centers.
3. The recreational/cultural attractiveness of downtown—its theaters, museums, sports events, fairs, or tourist attractions.
4. The accessibility, transportation, and parking convenience of downtown retail for the potential markets that it can serve.
5. The social character of downtown.
6. The extent, location, and character of existing retail facilities in downtown.
7. The availability and cost of land downtown.
8. The cost of construction and operations downtown.

The effect of one variable will depend on the conditions of eight or nine others and the interaction among them. For example, in most downtowns, parking is viewed to be a major problem for retail operations. There is not enough of it, it is expensive to construct and operate, shoppers often fear crime in parking structures, and fees drive customers away. Yet there are exceptions. The superstars of downtown retailing, in the opinion of one retail market analyst, are Manhattan, North Michigan Avenue in Chicago, and Union Square in San Francisco—all areas where parking is virtually unavailable or extremely expensive. Also, Faneuil Hall, one of the most success-ful of the contemporary downtown retailing projects, initially had little contiguous parking, illustrating that some factors can offset or override the influence of others.

The objective of a market assessment is to define the strengths and weaknesses of opportunities that are not being realized, but which *might* be solved through cooperative public and private ac-tion. In the assessment, the city should evaluate whether there are sufficient existing retail anchors that can provide the basis for a major new retail mall, or whether a shift in the location for optimal retailing calls for creation of an entirely new retail center, or whether tourist and convention business is or could be sufficient to support "festival" retailing such as that of Boston's Quincy Market or Baltimore's Harborplace.

Developers, investors, retailers—all should be consulted and involved in the assessment. They can tell the city whether the assessment is sound. In any event, their own views and their own situation must be part of any assessment.

The quality of this assessment is crucial to further planning.

Realistically assessing what the city can do   The assessment, if done well, will provide the city with an understanding of what opportunities there are to capture a larger share of the retail market and what is generally required to do so. It will identify problems to be overcome. And it will raise the questions of implementation. This places the ball in the court of the city government and downtown business and civic organizations. Two questions must be addressed:

1.   How willing are the city government and downtown business community to take steps to improve central city retailing?
2.   How effective can the city and downtown business and civic organizations be in coordinating and managing the downtown retail function as an integrated operation?

Developers and investors who sense that a leadership commitment is lacking or uncertain will not risk their time or money in working with the community.

There are downtown problems—physical, economic, and social—that can serve as obstacles to any retail development effort. Often downtown retail developments require management innovations comparable to those used in suburban malls. Sometimes the introduction of competition actually strengthens the pulling power of an existing store. The more diverse the shopping opportunities, the more customers are pulled in. The shopping center is a major social invention. By providing constant management over the retail area as a whole and by grouping shopping opportunities in close juxtaposition, a synergism among competing retailers results in which the sum is greater than the parts. Downtowns need to adapt this innovation to their own purposes.

There are added costs of doing business in many downtowns that can help make downtown retail development financially infeasible. Often, the only way to overcome these obstacles is through special incentives, concessions, or contributions to a retail development project that help make the financial arithmetic of a project come out right.

With limited public resources, cities are finding it advantageous and necessary to enter into new kinds of financial and business arrangements with private developers and financial institutions—arrangements which they had never previously contemplated, such as assuming the role of codeveloper.

Thus, in undertaking downtown retail development, a city must assess realistically what it can do. And the city, together with downtown business and civic leadership, must agree on the form and mechanism for ensuring close public and private cooperation in the formulation, planning, and execution of a retail development strategy.

Developing a basic retail development strategy   Once a general assessment of market opportunities and problems has been completed and an appropriate mechanism for close and stable public-private cooperation exists, a basic retail development strategy can be prepared and projects implemented.

What can the city do? Getting the civic act together

The *sine qua non* for a proposed downtown retail project, in the nearly unanimous opinion of the experts interviewed, is enthusiastic and aggressive local political and civic support. There are developers with much experience in downtown projects who will not consider going into a downtown project unless the city executive, the council, and the citizenry are demonstrably behind it. There are lenders who consider local government willingness to back a project as one of the key factors in their risk assessment. An almost universally cited worry of developers is that downtown projects can easily become political footballs. Therefore, they try to secure bipartisan support for proposals, or, preferably, to have at least day-to-day decisions removed from the political level and delegated to a nonpartisan, quasi-independent entity.

Downtown retail projects require an unusual amount of political and public support because they tend to be much more expensive and riskier to develop than their suburban competitors. As we have already seen, the additional expense and risk factors include land assembly problems, higher land costs, the need for parking structures, a longer development period, more stringent code requirements, and higher security and operating costs. Moreover, the success of a downtown retail project is more or less dependent on its physical or functional linkages with other downtown elements—offices, hotels, cultural or entertainment facilities, transit, and so forth. The forging of such links is of necessity a matter of cooperative arrangements between the project developer and the public sector and other business interests in the downtown.

In general, the city should expect to provide:

1. A sound and workable redevelopment or revitalization strategy and plan for downtown retail
2. Strong political support for the plan and its component projects

3. Assistance in site or property acquisition, if necessary
4. Financial support as required
5. Indirect support in the form of programs and policies to encourage the development of housing, amenities, and other attractions in and around the downtown that will help attract people to the area
6. A streamlined regulatory environment in which barriers to efficient financial and physical development are minimized.

Public-private cooperation   In addition to the public role, there is usually a need for a quasi-public body representing local interests and with financial powers that can provide financial support, stimulate private business and civic involvement in planning and decision making; carry out various entrepreneurial functions such as property acquisition, management, and development in an effective and expeditious manner; and provide financial participation when no other source is available. Projects in Philadelphia, Baltimore, Milwaukee, and San Diego have been carried out with the strong involvement of such quasi-public bodies.

In Philadelphia, for example, in order to minimize the risk to the developer, the Philadelphia Redevelopment Authority spent $18 million to build the shell for the Gallery retail project. In Baltimore, a quasi-public corporation, Charles Center/Inner Harbor, Inc., cleared the site and provided improved access and improved infrastructure for the highly successful Harborplace. The Milwaukee Redevelopment Corporation is a limited-profit corporation that can operate in a business-like manner to acquire land, work with consultants and city officials, and as any private developer, become directly involved in a project implementation.

Downtown retail management   The need for close public-private cooperation does not end with project development, however. One of the historical problems creating disadvantages for downtown retail relative to suburban malls has been the lack of effective central management. This problem has been recognized for some time, but it continues to plague most downtowns.

Under the "Main Street" program of the National Trust for Historic Preservation, there have been successes in providing voluntary coordination among merchants in some retail strips of smaller cities. A coordinator assigned to the project can assume responsibilities analogous to those of a suburban mall manager, but with these few exceptions, there is a lack of centralized management in downtown retail districts. Some of the retailers and developers interviewed were generally of the opinion that voluntary approaches to the creation of centralized management have not worked well. Many merchants are simply unwilling to cooperate.

The advantages of centralized management have been well

demonstrated: coordinated operating hours, control of tenant mix, common design themes, common and coordinated advertising, and so forth. Though centralized management is clearly advantageous and widely recognized as such, little has been done in most downtowns to solve the problems of decentralized retail operations. Thus, the most effective solution and course of least resistance appears to favor development of a new retail center under single ownership—a centrally managed facility.

This is an issue warranting concentrated attention. There are no legal means to impose involuntary controls on downtown merchants, at least to the degree necessary to control tenant mix and operating hours. Some cities have used special districts as a device to provide special maintenance, promotion, security, and transportation services in the downtown area. These districts are typically funded through a special property tax assessment on downtown property owners.

Although the model may not be replicated in most cities, it is reported that retail property owners in Schenectady, New York, formed a downtown retail corporation and transferred their individual properties to the corporation in exchange for an interest in it. The central corporation then obtained a central management capability.

The time has come when it may have been proven necessary to invent for many downtown retail districts management mechanisms and professional staff that can serve as both counterparts and competitors to those in suburban centers.

Public incentives and financing   Rare is the contemporary downtown large-scale retail project that has been developed without significant public subsidy or financing support. The following examples of direct public participation are instructive:

Charleston Town Center (Charleston, West Virginia)   Public funds being used to write down land costs, construct a garage, and help construct the shell of the mall.

Faneuil Hall (Boston, Massachusetts)   Public funds used for infrastructure improvements, property tax abatement, and advantageous (dollar-a-year) lease terms on the structure leased by the city to the developer.

Glendale Galleria (Glendale, California)   Public funds used to write down land costs, upgrade infrastructure, and build a garage.

The Grand Avenue (Milwaukee, Wisconsin)   Public funds used for public concourses, skyways, a parking structure, and underground utility improvements.

Harborplace (Baltimore, Maryland)   Public funds used to assemble and prepare land which is then leased to the project developer.

Lexington Center (Lexington, Kentucky)   Public funds used to develop an arena, convention center, the mall shell, and parking spaces.

Louisville Galleria (Louisville, Kentucky)   Public funds used to build parking, a department store, and portions of the mall.

Plaza Pasadena (Pasadena, California)   Public funds used for site acquisition and preparation and parking construction.

Most cities can expect to provide one or more of the following if a major downtown retail development project is to prove feasible:

1. Necessary improvements to streets and freeways to improve access and general environment
2. Subsidized parking
3. Acquisition and preparation of sites for new construction
4. Expeditious approvals of rezonings, street realignments, and the like
5. Legislation to allow the establishment of special downtown management organizations financed by special exactions
6. Financial assistance in the form of "soft" loans or "soft" leases for facilities
7. Obtaining state and federal financial assistance when available through urban development action grant or other grant programs
8. Providing financial assistance for the development of downtown housing.

Such substantial front-end public subsidies frequently become a matter of some controversy. Some observers argue that city returns should be accounted for by spinoffs such as increased employment, tax revenues, and the project's attraction of additional real estate investment to the area. This school thinks cities should stay out of the direct risk and profit aspects of the real estate business.

On the other hand, others point out that many recent projects have easily repaid the public investment in the project in a few years. Boston, for example, invested approximately $12 million in Faneuil Hall and has received well over $2 million per year in lease payments alone.

Other observers feel quite strongly that cities should structure business deals with developers in an effort to recover and even make a profit on their front-end subsidies. Municipalities as investors have participated in a good number of recent retail projects by receiving lease or cash flow income from the project (Faneuil Hall, the

Grand Avenue, Harborplace, the Louisville Galleria, Rainbow Centre in Niagara Falls, the Gallery in Philadelphia) or parking revenues (Charleston Town Center, Plaza Pasadena, the Gallery in Philadelphia).

The precise form and participation of the city is very much an element in its basic strategy for downtown retail development.

The triangular partnership Each partner in the development project, in addition to the local government, has special responsibilities.

The developer is the director and organizer of the process. He conceptualizes the project, initiates activity, assumes risk, invests money, and expects to earn a profit in return. When the local government is involved as codeveloper, it assists the developer in some of these responsibilities and correspondingly must share some of the risks.

The third group of participants in a development project are the investors and lenders. The developer is responsible for seeking out organizations or individuals willing to invest money in the project. These "equity investors" can expect three types of return: cash flow, tax benefits, and/or capital appreciation. Many projects are organized as limited partnerships. A limited partnership consists of two kinds of partners: the general partner, normally the active member of the organization, has unlimited liability and must bear responsibility for any commitments or debts entered into by the partnership. Limited partners, on the other hand, are liable only up to a designated amount, usually the amount of their investment.

Lenders also have two important responsibilities in development projects: first, they are the source of debt financing; second, they carefully review a project's economic and financial feasibility. Almost every lender requires an economic feasibility study for any project. Lenders provide several sources of capital: construction loans that help cover construction and some front-end costs; and permanent financing for a completed project.

The local government, developer, and investors/lenders comprise a triangular development partnership, but civic organizations also become a vital part of the equation in most cities. Without broad-based support from civic organizations few projects can succeed. Active opposition will kill the chances for most major projects to either be implemented or succeed if they are.

Urban Infill:
Its Potential As a
Development
Strategy

Real Estate Research Corporation

Urban infill has been the subject of much interest on the part of both the public and private sectors in recent years. Central cities and mature suburban communities have begun to recognize its importance as a strategy in their development arsenal. Likewise, developers and builders have begun to realize its profit potential. Despite this interest, little has actually been known about infill land: its magnitude, its characteristics, or its potential.

Recognizing this lack of information, the U.S. Department of Housing and Urban Development commissioned Real Estate Research Corporation (RERC) to undertake a comprehensive analysis of infill opportunities and constraints. The primary focus was detailed case studies of infill parcels and their development potential in three diverse metropolitan counties—Dade County (Miami, Florida); King County (Seattle); and Monroe County (Rochester, New York).

In all, approximately 500 parcels were examined in terms of their size, ownership, zoning, physical characteristics, availability for development, neighborhood dynamics, and marketability. A comparative study was also made of development costs on infill sites and at the urban fringe. Although generalizations about national potential or about development economics certainly cannot be made on the basis of three in-depth case studies, especially for a

Reprinted with permission of the Real Estate Research Corporation. This executive summary was prepared as part of a study commissioned by the Office of Policy Development and Research, U.S. Department of Housing and Urban Development, October 1981. The original contains additional figures and photographs that illustrate the text.

phenomenon as multifaceted as infill, commonalities emerged in the three metropolitan areas that provide guidance for cities and developers alike.

This summary highlights some of these findings without explaining the detailed research methodology. Several companion volumes present in-depth findings, quantitative analyses, and descriptive guidelines for inventorying local infill potential and stimulating development on available parcels.

Identifying infill land

Simply stated, infill land consists of vacant parcels that are already served by utilities and are surrounded by urban development.

A wide spectrum of infill parcels was examined in the three case studies, ranging from lots suitable only for individual homes to bypassed tracts of 20 acres or more. These sites were both privately and publicly owned, located in built-up suburbs as well as central cities, and carried any zoning or planning designation other than permanent open space. As long as the parcels were within already urbanized areas and served by (or close to) water and sewer lines, they were considered as part of the infill land supply.

Every city in the country contains land that has remained vacant despite successive waves of development. This evolutionary process is illustrated in Figure 1, which shows the sequential stages by which land becomes urbanized and available for development.

How large is the supply of infill land? How much of that land is usable? How much new development could it support? The answers will vary among metropolitan areas and within individual cities or suburbs, but untapped opportunities exist in virtually every community.

Our research indicates that significant quantities of infill land free of environmental constraints exist in most regions—and in attractive locations. Whether this land supply is, in and of itself, sufficient to handle projected future growth is important but somewhat academic. In some areas it could be sufficient; in others it will not be. Of greater concern is whether builders will find it profitable to use the infill land supply that exists, and whether local governments will create an environment that encourages builder interest.

Market trends encourage infill

Infill locations may not capture all of a region's demand for vacant land, but they should be able to attract a far larger share than they have in the past. A number of urban market trends now favor centrality, and developers are looking at developed as well as developing areas. Simultaneously, local governments are interested in increasing their tax bases without further expanding their infrastructures. Thus, as demonstrated by the 15 points listed in

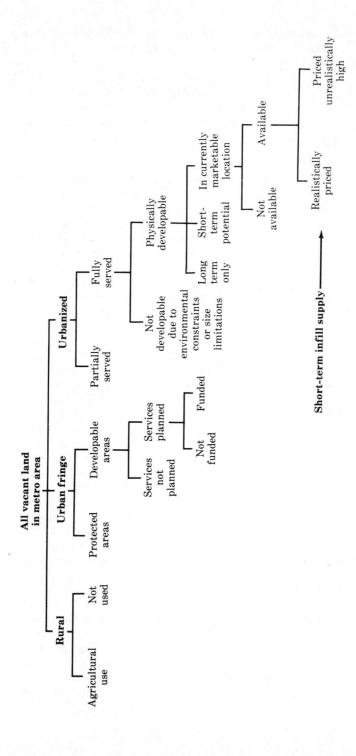

Figure 1. The vacant land continuum.

Figure 2, contemporary market and fiscal trends favor infilling.

Two real estate "givens" underlie development direction at any particular juncture:

1. The key to success in real estate development is location, location, location.
2. Timing is everything.

In combination, the point is that developers are looking for the right project at the right site at the right time. The times are auspicious for infill because continued outward growth is slowing in many metropolitan areas, environmental and fiscal constraints discourage raw land from being urbanized, and individuals and businesses are increasingly attracted to accessible, closer-in locations.

Infill development should not be viewed as a panacea that will accommodate all future growth. Infill potential can vary significantly among metropolitan areas, as suggested in Figure 3. Building will continue at the urban fringe, but at a slower pace than in the '50s, '60s, and '70s. Rehabilitation and redevelopment of underuti-

1. Rising energy costs reinforce the advantages of close-in locations

2. Decreasing capability of local governments to expand infrastructure at the urban fringe

3. Escalating costs of land preparation at the urban fringe

4. Increasing interest in public transit accessibility

5. Growing costs in money, time, and "aggravation" of obtaining approvals for development on raw land

6. Rising local government need for tax base expansion

7. Strengthening service economy and growth in centrally-located office employment

8. Declining proportion of child-oriented households

9. Rising interest in accessibility to urban amenities and multiple uses

10. Expanding multiuse nodes in cities and suburbs

11. Increasing scrutiny of excess land in public ownership

12. Growing pressures to preserve environmentally sensitive or agricultural land

13. Need to maximize use of inplace public facilities

14. Strengthening of older neighborhoods through preservation and rehabilitation efforts

15. Capitalizing on development opportunities that do not require substantial public expenditure

Figure 2. Trends encouraging infill development.

Factors	Markets with highest potential	Markets with lowest potential
Growth	Rapidly growing population; extensive demand for new housing	No population growth; limited new household formation
Employment centers	Strong CBD and local employment nodes; long commuting distances from the urban fringe	Weak CBD; dispersed employment centers; short commutes from the fringe to jobs
Building conditions	Extensive investment (public and private) in neighborhood preservation and upgrading	Little investment in existing building stock or public facilities
Resident incomes	Infill land located in a variety of neighborhoods serving many income groups	Infill land concentrated in low-income neighborhoods
Land prices	Shallow land price gradient from urban fringe to inner city or significant density differences to balance steep gradient	Steep land price gradient from urban fringe to inner city and little variation in land use densities
Growth controls	Limits on outward spread of development operating regionwide	No growth guidance or coordination among jurisdictions
Availability and cost of services	Developers at the fringe pay costs of service extensions and assist with school and park requirements; limited preservicing	Extensive preservicing; little in the way of impact fees charged

Figure 3. Factors affecting infill potential.

lized land will also capture a significant share of development demand. However, public officials willing to promote their infill inventories should encounter positive responses from the real estate community. Unlike many historic urban development programs that sought to counter trends, infill activity is very much in the mainstream of developer interest and supports current trends.

Being realistic, infill also faces obstacles:

1. Land costs may be high.
2. Parcels are generally small.
3. Many sites are being held off the market by the owners.
4. Neighbors may resist new construction, especially if zoning changes are involved.

Oftentimes, the obstacles can be mitigated, and tools for doing that are listed in Figure 5.

Infill land characteristics

Magnitude of opportunities   In total acreage, vacant infill land represents 37,000 acres in urbanized Miami (Dade County), 70,000 acres in Seattle (King County), and 66,000 acres in Rochester (Monroe County). After eliminating clearly nonresidential sites, property currently unavailable for development, and parcels with physical or market limitations, RERC found that there are approximately 10,000 acres of residential infill land in Miami, 24,000 acres in Seattle, and 13,000 acres in Rochester.

These properties could theoretically accommodate two-thirds of Miami's, nearly all of Seattle's, and all of Rochester's residential growth for the next 10 years. It would not be advisable, however, to force all future growth onto these sites because there is also a market need for development at the urban fringe. To avoid unacceptable inflation of land prices, the market must remain competitive in terms of locational choice and quantity of supply.

Parcel size and assembly potential   Infill parcels range from less than one-quarter acre to 20 acres or more. There are relatively few individual parcels with more than five acres. Over half the lots in all three areas are a quarter acre or less—the equivalent of the average single-family detached home site. The size patterns are similar from city to city, but there are more smaller parcels in the Miami area, which has the strongest and highest value real estate market of the three. Clearly, there has already been intense development pressure on the larger parcels that existed five or ten years ago.

The capacity of small infill parcels to meet market demand may be substantially enhanced by land assembly. In Seattle and Rochester, between 50 percent and 60 percent of the sampled infill parcels were observed to be adjacent to other vacant land. In Miami, infill sites are slightly more isolated, with only 40 percent bordered by another undeveloped property. Most of this land is not in single ownership. RERC staff also found numerous instances where infill parcels abutted underutilized properties that could be redeveloped in conjunction with a project on the vacant site next door. Consolidating infill parcels into larger, more easily developable sites will, in most cases, call for coordinated land assembly involving multiple owners. This adds to the complexity of development but may increase the rewards as well.

Physical attributes   The vast majority of infill sites are free of severe physical limitations to development. Certain vacant sites—such as remnants from highway construction or long but narrow abandoned rights-of-way—will not be developable. Other limitations, such as steep slopes or flood prone locations, can be corrected through careful design. New site planning and construction techniques are enhancing the attractiveness of difficult-to-develop parcels that were "skipped over" ten or even five years ago. However, sensitive sites cannot be developed at the same densities that are possible for unconstrained land; per unit construction costs can be high.

Infrastructure conditions Although infill sites, by definition, have access to roads, utilities, and other public services, their condition or capacity is not always adequate to support new development—especially large-scale, high-density projects. For example, 15 percent of the sampled infill parcels in urbanized King County lack direct frontage on public roads. In Dade County, one-third of the sites have public water lines with diameters smaller than the standard 6 inches needed to maintain adequate pressure and fire flow for development at urban densities. It is not uncommon to find water and sewer lines that are over 50 years old serving infill parcels.

Maintenance practices vary considerably among jurisdictions. Fiscal limitations, especially in older central cities, result in deferred spending on capital upgrading and replacement. These problems need public attention, not only to encourage infilling but also to stimulate and reinforce investment in existing buildings in older neighborhoods.

Zoning In all metropolitan areas, some degree of "mismatch" exists between market demand and the zoning designations of the vacant land supply. Communities "over zone" for industrial or commercial uses in the hope of attracting tax ratables. Multi-family housing, which can make efficient use of expensive infill sites, is often viewed as less desirable than low-density single-family homes, especially in the suburbs.

In a rapidly changing real estate market, it is impossible to achieve a perfect balance between zoning and the demand for land. Community preferences must also be considered. Nevertheless, inappropriate zoning can be a deterrent to infilling. Of the owners of available infill properties interviewed as part of this study, roughly 25 percent in all three case studies felt that some change in existing zoning would improve the marketability of their land. In weak markets, downzoning is suggested as a way of reducing artificially high land prices. In desirable areas, density bonuses may be needed to make development more economical. Modifying site planning standards for sideyards, setbacks, and off-street parking can also be helpful.

Location of infill lots In all three urban counties examined, a majority of infill lots are located in the suburbs. Lots in Miami/Miami Beach accounted for only 28 percent of all infill parcels; for Seattle, the central city share was 41 percent. Lots in the city of Rochester were more numerous, accounting for 47 percent of the total. City lots are often clustered in low-income neighborhoods, thereby limiting their marketability.

More important is the considerable size disparity between infill parcels in central cities and those in the suburbs. Suburban sites are far larger. As a result, they account for over 90 percent of the infill acreage in all three cases. If unconstrained by zoning or physical limitations, these larger suburban tracts will be more readily marketable.

Land ownership   Infill land is owned by a multiplicity of small-scale entrepreneurs and private citizens. In all three metro areas, more than half of the sample parcels are held by private individuals. Business entities control far fewer of the vacant parcels than many observers would expect. Government owners are overrepresented in the Monroe County sample because many vacant properties there are tax delinquent or were cleared years ago by the Rochester Urban Renewal Authority. If government properties are excluded from the inventories, the proportion of parcels in individual (as opposed to business) ownership is 69 percent in Monroe County and 71 percent in the Seattle area. This means that of privately held sites, about two-thirds are controlled by individual citizens.

Only one-fourth of the infill parcels examined in RERC's investigation are owned by people who are engaged primarily in the real estate business. Speculators who purposefully hold property off the market are not the dominant holders of vacant urban land. However, major corporations or institutions can control the larger properties that are most attractive to the typical big suburban builders.

The vast majority of infill parcels are owned by individuals and businesses located within the metropolitan area—not foreigners or corporations located in another part of the country. Ownership by outsiders accounts for less than one-fifth of all parcels.

Land availability   Not all of the infill land supply is available for development. In fact, just over half of the approximately 500 parcels surveyed are or would be on the market within five years. Availability of land is highest in Rochester (62 percent); whereas in Seattle and Miami, the figures are 50 percent and 53 percent respectively.

The real estate knowledge and sophistication of infill land owners vary considerably. However, owners of sites who would make their properties available for development voice strong optimism about future development potential. Fully half to three-quarters of infill site owners believe that the market for their land will improve over the next five years. This may help to explain the fact that only half of all privately owned infill sites are currently available for purchase.

Owner motives   Motivations for property ownership are difficult to isolate, but RERC's research suggests that there are three dominant reasons for holding infill land:

1. Future appreciation/investment—the primary motivating force for both individuals and businesses.
2. Personal use—most significant for vacant parcels adjacent to existing residences.
3. Future expansion—providing future reserves for both business and residential development. This is also the motivation for government agencies' retention of land for anticipated facility needs, though some of those needs may no longer exist in cities with stable or declining populations.

The properties being held for appreciation or investment, and some of those reserved for expansion, could be made available for development, given positive market conditions, workable financing, and "the right price." Overall, about half the parcels examined could be deemed available.

Land prices and housing costs   Infill land in stable, middle-income neighborhoods can be as much as 15 times as expensive, on an average per unit basis, as raw land at the metropolitan fringe. Statistical averages mask important realities within any market area. High land prices are a function of desirability (quality of the surrounding neighborhood, absence of development obstacles, and perceived market strength).

New infrastructure costs can be significantly less for infill housing than for identical units at the suburban fringe, but the savings will usually be insufficient to offset higher land prices in stable mature neighborhoods. Small infill parcels that can make maximum use of existing in-place utilities will have minimal site improvement costs. Larger infill projects require creation of on-site roads and utilities, so their costs per dwelling unit will not be dramatically lower than for development at the urban fringe.

High land prices, per se, will not necessarily limit development. The key factor is what can be built and sold or rented on the land and the relationship between sales prices or rental rates and land cost. In other words, the developer will pay high land prices if the final package of land and building will command high rents or a high sales price.

For housing consumers, price parity is often achieved between central-city and fringe locations when commuting and total transportation costs are taken into account. For example, an average household living at the urban fringe in Rochester could be expected to spend $3,100 more per year on commuting and auto ownership than the same household in the city of Rochester. This equation is being considered more and more as energy costs escalate.

Neighborhood attitudes   City governments that want to encourage infill will have to anticipate, plan for, and resolve conflicts between builders and local interest groups. One of the most common neighborhood concerns is compatibility of new building design with the surrounding structures. Sensitive design solutions are often possible—using similar facades and setbacks, for example. However, if the initial proposal is for a wrenchingly incompatible structure, nearby property owners may be righteously indignant and force expensively unpleasant confrontations.

Residents and local business owners may be extremely aware of aging sewer and water systems that lack the capacity to handle additional loads or to withstand the jarring of heavy construction. Again, opposition can be reduced if the city and/or developer address these problems first.

In middle-income neighborhoods—especially those that have recently been upgraded through the initiative of individual homeowners—infilling may be opposed because the new structures will generate more traffic, exacerbate parking problems, or introduce an incompatible scale or design. In low-income neighborhoods, residents may view infilling as the beginning of gentrification and displacement—depending on the type of development proposed.

Many developers who are accustomed to building at the urban fringe are extremely apprehensive about neighborhood protests. Thus, they look to local governments for help in obtaining approvals and mitigating neighborhood opposition.

Roles for local government

Efficient processing can go a long way in allaying builders' fears and creating a positive environment for development. This is particularly important, given the fact that most infill parcels are small and therefore appeal to the small- or medium-sized developer. Such individuals and companies typically have limited staff time and are relatively inexperienced in dealing with a wide range of government agencies. Because time is money in development, expediting permit processing is essential.

As interest in infill heightens, local public agencies should take steps to identify, classify, and become familiar with vacant parcels within their jurisdictions. Most local governments remain only vaguely aware of the location and extent of skipped-over properties.

Infill is a fairly new concept and most developers are not actively scrutinizing urban areas to locate individual buildable parcels. Cities can prepare inventories and market analyses for available sites, particularly those that fit the general description in Figure 4, and then distribute the information to local real estate brokers and developers.

Local agencies also play an important role in determining project feasibility, mainly through traditional activities such as

The context	The property
Viable market area	For sale at realistic price
Compatible, well-maintained surrounding properties	Sufficient size for intended use
Receptive neighborhood	Perceived market for intended use(s)
Helpful city government	Adequate utilities in place
Absence of environmental problems	Street frontage
Workable building code	Regularly-shaped developable parcels
Good public services	No major topographic, drainage or subsoil problem
	Appropriate zoning
	Potential development profitability comparable to alternative sites

Figure 4. The optimum infill site.

zoning and planning reviews and by capital investment programs to build roads, sewers and water mains. Techniques that can be used to encourage infilling range from "passive" efforts at technical assistance (for both builders and neighborhood groups) to modified codes and review procedures or more conscious targeting of capital improvements. Creative liaison with neighborhood groups that oppose new construction projects is emerging as a legitimate public activity. Other techniques being used to encourage rehabilitation and redevelopment—such as tax abatement or tax increment financing—can also be used to assist infill projects.

These and other techniques that have been used in specific localities and are suitable for encouragement of infill are listed in Figure 5. The list is representative rather than comprehensive, and few of the techniques are unique to infill usage. Most of them are familiar to city planners and building officials, but they may not have been targeted as yet to this application.

Reconciling the competing concerns of private developers, neighboring property owners and local governments is not an easy task. But there is ample evidence that it can work, and that market conditions are now more favorable for infilling than they have been in the last 20 years. Opportunities are available for the private sector to make a profit while acting in concert with public goals for sound urban development.

Needed actions	Possible incentives	Target opportunities	Cautions
Stimulating developer interest in infilling	Training programs/seminars/publicity campaign	Outreach to builders, developers, and realtors through professional associations and the news media	May have to go outside the region for speakers who have had success with infilling
	Parcel files; information on prototype projects	Comprehensive; or only for special uses (multi-family; industrial)	Needs careful staff supervision
	Design competitions	For scattered small lots; for large areas offering unique opportunities	Needs volunteers to serve on review committees and needs funds for prizes
Removing obstacles created by government			
Reducing delays in project review	Reform of staff review procedures	Small-scale projects	Must assure adequate citizen participation
	Elimination of unnecessary hearings	Projects requiring variances or special use permits	Requires cooperation of many city departments and staff members
	Creation of ombudsman or expeditor	All projects; or just those involving assisted housing or employment generation	Obstacles in state enabling legislation
Correcting excessively high or inappropriate standards	Reexamination of code provisions; encouragement of performance-based requirements	All infill projects; could also be important in redevelopment and rehabilitation	May encounter resistance from city staff, building trades, or neighborhood groups; results will not be immediately visible
Improving zoning balance (not enough multi-family land; over-zoning for industrial use)	Comprehensive review of zoning map and/or regulations	Citywide or in designated neighborhoods as part of the neighborhood planning process	May encounter resistance from neighborhood residents and property owners depending on the types of changes proposed. Must be based on sound market analysis

Figure 5. Tools and techniques for encouraging infilling.

Needed actions	Possible incentives	Target opportunities	Cautions
Creating neighborhood support for infilling	Inclusion in neighborhood plans of strategies for dealing with vacant lots	All neighborhoods (especially those with high potential)	Neighbors must see advantages for existing housing and businesses as well as the developer if they are to be convinced; developers must be flexible and willing to listen
	Project review meetings with developer in advance of official hearings	All projects likely to generate controversy	May also need to meet neighborhood groups in advance
Addressing market weakness or uncertainty/poor area image	Demonstration projects involving local development corporations and neighborhood interests	Low- and moderate-income neighborhoods, especially for projects providing jobs and/or increased shopping or services	Builds confidence if successful; high risk; limited expertise in dealing with risky situations
	Loan guarantees	Projects in areas with poor image but location advantages (i.e., near jobs, transit, major institutions)	Risk of unsuccessful projects requires expertise of experienced builders and banks
	"Below-market" financing through mortgage revenue bonds or industrial bond programs	Target neighborhoods and projects where special financing terms can act as a "magnet" to households or businesses who would otherwise locate at the urban fringe	Recent federal legislative limitations; need for careful market studies
	Greater attention to maintenance and rehabilitation	Low- and moderate-income neighborhoods	Concern over long-term displacement of the poor
	Visible public commitment to upgrading public works	Target neighborhoods	Resistance to targeting on a neighborhood basis
	Interim uses (parking, gardens, play areas)	Areas with established neighborhood organizations that will assume maintenance responsibility; areas with open space or parking needs	High maintenance burdens; resistance to future change

Figure 5. Tools and techniques for encouraging infilling (continued).

Addressing site-specific problems			
Reducing the high cost of infill land	Land price write-down	Unique opportunity to achieve public purpose	High costs if used extensively; adverse political impacts from using public funds to subsidize strictly private projects
	Tax abatement	Definite project with committed developer	
	Leasing of publicly owned land	Varies; generally used for housing developments priced for low/moderate-income occupancy	Careful lease structuring needed to protect public interest
	Density bonuses; permitting variances from sideyards or setbacks to allow greater coverage	Mixed-use projects; projects incorporating assisted housing	Need to assure design compatibility with surrounding areas; possible opposition of neighbors
	Forgiveness of delinquent back taxes	Definite projects with committed developers	Legal obstacles in some states
	Downzoning	Areas where permitted densities do not match local housing market preferences	Objections of landowners
	Fee waivers	All infill projects	Fees are not a high proportion of project costs; effects are more psychological than financial
Increasing land availability	Property tax "disincentives" —site value taxation —higher taxes on vacant land	Vacant land in marketable locations (targeting will be difficult if not impossible)	Adverse effects on vacant property owners in deteriorated areas; adverse effects on existing buildings in "hot" neighborhoods
	Land assembly (vacant land only or vacant and underutilized sites)	Definite projects with committed developers	Expensive; legal limitations on use of eminent domain powers

Figure 5. Tools and techniques for encouraging infilling (continued).

Needed actions	Possible incentives	Target opportunities	Cautions
Increasing land availability *(continued)*	Land banking	Areas with extensive scattered parcels; high incidence of tax delinquency	Expensive; may require enabling legislation; land may not be marketable in the short run, especially in weak markets
Correcting infrastructure problems	Public funding of off-site capital improvements (minor street and utility extensions or upgrading)	Small-scale infilling, especially for industrial use	Reluctance of elected officials to target limited CIP dollars to new development; need for flexibility in CIP administration
	Tax increment financing	Larger projects, especially mixed use	Legal limitations in most states
	Special improvement districts	Commercial and industrial areas covering both infill and rehabilitation	Taxpayers must be willing to participate
	Greater flexibility and creativity in plan review	All infill projects	Resistance from city public works/ engineering staff to deviation from "standards"

Figure 5. Tools and techniques for encouraging infilling (continued)

High-Technology Development: Local Initiatives

Office of Technology Assessment

A wide range of programs have been developed by state governments and universities to encourage high-technology development (HTD), and initiatives have been launched by local governments and community organizations as well. These local programs usually arise from the specific needs and goals of particular communities, whereas state programs may not always be appropriate or useful for individual cities or regions. University programs, on the other hand, usually focus on improving linkages with the local business community. Consequently, the success of state and university programs often is affected by the presence or absence of these local initiatives.

The Office of Technology Assessment (OTA) identified and analyzed a representative cross section of local HTD initiatives in order to determine what types of programs have been attempted, how well they have worked, and the factors that affect their effectiveness and their transferability to other communities. The material in this article is based on interviews with community representatives and detailed investigation of 54 separate high-technology initiatives in the following 22 communities: Huntsville, Ala.; Phoenix, Ariz.; San Diego, Calif.; Colorado Springs, Colo.; Brevard County, Fla.; Orlando, Fla.; Chicago, Ill.; Lowell, Mass.; Montgomery County, Md.; Minneapolis–St. Paul, Minn.; Albuquerque, N. Mex.; Binghamton, N.Y.; Cincinnati, Ohio; Portland, Oreg.; Philadelphia, Pa.; Oak

Reprinted from *Technology, Innovation, and Regional Economic Development*, background paper no. 2, *Encouraging High-Technology Development*, prepared by the Office of Technology Assessment of the U.S. Congress. Material in this article is based on the contractor report, *Local High-Technology Initiatives Study*, prepared for OTA by the Fantus Co., Charles Ford Harding, principal investigator, April 1983.

Ridge, Tenn.; Austin, Tex.; San Antonio, Tex.; Salt Lake City, Utah; Burlington, Vt.; Seattle, Wash.; and Milwaukee, Wis.

Community typology

Substate and local efforts to stimulate HTD are driven by the increased jobs and tax base that would result for local economies. In deciding to focus on HTD as opposed to other possible avenues, the communities are generally influenced by the rapid growth of technology-based industry compared to other sectors of the economy and by the tremendous contributions that high-technology companies have made to the local economies of Silicon Valley and the Boston area. The use of these areas as models for development is made clear by efforts of communities to promote themselves as "Silicon Mountain," "Silicon Coast," or "Silicon Plain." Thus, one useful typology of communities is in the degree to which they vary from these model communities.

Indeed, OTA found that many local initiatives can be described as strategies used to develop the characteristics of the model communities. The type and importance of the resulting initiatives will depend, in part, on the principal shortcomings that community leaders believe are keeping their city from being a center of HTD like Santa Clara County or the Boston area. Using this criterion as the principal means of classifying cities, OTA has identified five types of communities:

1. High-technology centers
2. Diluted high-technology centers
3. Spillover communities
4. Technology installation centers
5. Bootstrap communities.

High-technology centers   Typified by Santa Clara County and the Boston area, these communities already have a high concentration of research-oriented companies and a major research-oriented university (Stanford and Massachusetts Institute of Technology). The large companies and universities, in turn, continually spin off other small companies, generally founded by researchers who have an idea for a product that they choose to develop on their own rather than within the environment of the larger firm. While some of these new companies fail, enough succeed and grow to increase the concentration of firms in the area.

Other important elements of the high-technology centers include a skilled work force, a university catering to the continuing education needs of local researchers, and the availability of venture capital. The skilled work force is trained by the large companies located in the area. The demands that these companies and their smaller counterparts make on the labor market encourage local workers to develop skills in technological areas; demand also makes it worthwhile for local vocational/technical schools to develop appropriate training programs. The depth of the local base of skilled workers, in turn, makes it possible for entrepreneurs to hire employees they might not otherwise have the resources to train.

Due to the rapid change of technology, engineers and technical workers at the technology-based companies must study constantly to keep abreast of their fields of interest. Others may take courses outside their fields of specialization. In both cases, many workers find it valuable to be able to continue their education in evening programs at nearby universities. Interestingly, in both Boston and Santa Clara County, this service is not provided by the major research university: the largest number of continuing education students in Boston attend Northeastern University, while in Silicon Valley they attend the University of Santa Clara.

Finally, the rapid growth of smaller companies with new products attracts the development of venture capital firms that specialize in identifying and providing capital and managerial advice to new and expanding technology-based companies. It is not surprising that, between 1970 and 1980, Massachusetts and California were the only states that consistently attracted a positive inflow of venture capital.

One problem for the high-technology centers, however, is that they tend to export many of the jobs that are generated through the innovations of local companies. The rapid growth of local firms tends to push up land and labor costs, and—at the point in a product's lifecycle when it no longer requires the highly skilled work force—the company will have a strong incentive to export its production to a lower cost area while concentrating the energies of the skilled work force on the innovations that require their talents. A community that exports its technologies must continually develop new ones to keep its economy healthy.

Diluted high-technology centers   These cities also have a base of large technology-oriented companies, skilled work forces, research universities, and venture capital firms. But in these cases, the high-technology orientation of the area is diluted in larger, broader, and more mature economies. Metropolitan areas such as New York and Chicago typify this group of communities.

The Chicago area, for example, possesses most of the characteristics of a high-technology center, including: *major research institutions* (University of Chicago, Northwestern University, Illinois Institute of Technology, University of Illinois at Chicago, Fermi National Labs, and Argonne National Labs); *major technology-based companies* (Baxter-Travenol Labs, G. D. Searle, Abbott Labs, Motorola, Gould, Northrop, and others); *continuing education courses in science and engineering* (offered at the Illinois Institute of Technology); *vocational/technical training* (offered at several two-year community colleges in the area); and *venture capital* (provided by venture capital firms and the Continental and First National banks). However, these high-technology characteristics are diluted in Chicago's much broader economy, many parts of which are unrelated to high technology.

This dilution seems to reduce the innovative and entrepreneurial fervor of an area. In such an area, skilled workers are more likely to be lost to nontechnological endeavors, and universities are more likely to support a broader set of community needs. In addition, venture capital firms may be less likely to specialize in new businesses based on technological innovation. Consequently, a major focus of high-technology initiatives in such areas has been to increase the communication among the various participants in HTD in the area. Thus, the high-technology newsletter in Chicago and the University City Science Center in Philadelphia are seen by those who developed them as a means of bringing the high-technology players in the community together and making them aware of local resources that they might not otherwise find. It is reasonable to perceive these efforts as attempts to overcome the effects of dilution.

Spillover communities   Spillover communities are those located adjacent to a high-technology center or diluted centers. While these communities typically lack most or all of the ingredients that make up a high-technology center, they are close enough to such a city to take advantage of its resources. A high-technology company located in such a community can exploit the research capabilities at the nearby universities, visit venture capital firms easily, and hire engineers and scientists from the large technical work force around the high-technology center and within commuting distance. Employees seeking graduate courses in their field can commute to universities in the adjacent city. Typically, the objective of such communities is to capture the spillover of companies from the center looking for lower cost land and a less competitive labor market. Three examples of this type of community are Lowell, Mass.; Naperville, Ill.; and Montgomery County, Md.

Lowell provides a particularly instructive case. With the exception of a university, the community lacked most of the ingredients of a high-technology center, but it is located adjacent to the Boston area. Through careful land-use planning, the city was able to induce Wang Laboratories to locate a plant in the area. Later, when Wang was looking for a new headquarters site, the community successfully pursued and won it with aggressive initiatives. Wang has since contributed to the further growth of high-technology infrastructure and the creation of new firms in the area.

For communities located adjacent to a high-technology center, this type of strategy has obvious appeal. They often must overcome perceptions of distance and an older image that may not be compatible with a high-technology firm. Lowell's success at overcoming its "mill-town" reputation shows that this can be done. A principal means of doing this is by creating a physical environment attractive to technology-based companies.

Technology installation centers   These communities are the home of a major research or technology-based institution, but they lack most or all of the other ingredients of a high-technology center. The installation creates a local base of researchers and skilled workers, and in some cases, this has led to extensive spinoff activities in the local economy. In other cases, however, the technical base created by the research installation produces few new firms and often remains unavailable to new employers coming into the area. This is because pay scales are usually quite high at such operations; additionally, the organization's rules regarding the rights to innovations have sometimes made it difficult for its research staff to start companies of their own.

As a result, local development initiatives often are begun after a downturn in the fortunes or funding of the major research installation. Thus, layoffs at Boeing in Seattle, program cutbacks at the Kennedy Space Center in Brevard County, Fla., and staff reductions at the Redstone Arsenal in Huntsville, Ala., all resulted in intensified development efforts, usually directed at technology-based companies that could take advantage of the skilled work force released by the installation.

These problems do not always apply, however, and the installations also attract a wide variety of suppliers that could be useful to other technology-based enterprises. For this reason, and because of the prestige associated with them, competition for such installations is usually intense, as was the case before the Microelectronics & Computer Technology Corp. (MCC) chose to locate in Austin, Tex., after considering over 50 candidate communities. Several communities are seeking to attract or establish such installations in the hope that this will attract others from outside the area and, eventually, lead to the creation of new, indigenous technology-based firms.

Bootstrap communities   A number of communities began their development efforts possessing none of the characteristics of the high-technology centers. They have depended instead on low operating costs and attractive living environments to attract the expansion plants of high-technology companies. These branch plants generally manufacture products which no longer have a high technological input; at this stage in their life cycle, competitive operating costs are far more important than the research capabilities of a high-technology center. However, when several of these plants have located in an area, their combined work forces create a pool of skilled labor that a more sophisticated operation can build upon. Additionally, the combined engineering work forces at such plants create enough demand to merit the addition or improvement of engineering and science courses at local universities.

As these things occur, the community is able to attract increasingly sophisticated operations and, eventually, foster the creation of local spinoffs. Communities that fall into this pattern include Austin, Colorado Springs, Orlando, Phoenix, and San Antonio. These cities have enjoyed rapid job growth from new branch plants of technology-based companies. Interestingly, two of the most recent announcements of new facilities in Austin were the research laboratories of Lockheed Corp. and MCC. Although the growth of a local base of "indigenous" high-technology firms has been slower, it too has been impressive.

Initiatives in these communities generally focus on developing the technical infrastructure and institutional linkages that will permit progressive increases in the technological sophistication of new facilities in the area. Such initiatives include the development or improvement of engineering courses at local universities, the addition of vocational/technical courses to provide workers with needed skills, and the development of research parks to create the environment desired by technology-based firms.

Implications for local initiatives   As one would expect, not all cities fit neatly into this typology. Minneapolis–St. Paul, for example, fits somewhere between the true high-technology centers and the diluted centers. Cincinnati, on the other hand, has some of the characteristics of a diluted center, but its high-technology base is limited; its development efforts have focused on creating a research installation, developing a venture capital fund, and increasing the flow of technological information among local machine tool companies. The value of the typology is not that any one city fits it neatly, but rather that by determining which type a city most closely approximates, it can launch the initiative that will be most appropriate and effective in developing a more sophisticated technological base.

A word of caution, however, is in order. Before deciding upon a high-technology program, a community should investigate other approaches to development that might result in a greater return on its investment. Not all communities can expect to enjoy rapid growth from high-technology operations. For example, OTA experienced difficulty in identifying small rural communities with effective initiatives; this suggests that relatively few such towns will receive direct benefits in jobs and taxes from high-technology plants.

Common initiatives

Some of the most common types of initiatives used by substate and local organizations to attract high-technology industry include the following:

1. Land use, planning, and zoning
2. University improvements
3. Vocational-technical training
4. Incubator buildings
5. Marketing programs
6. High-technology task forces
7. Venture capital funds.

Land use, planning, and zoning   High-technology firms generally are quite concerned about the quality of the environment in which they are located. They want land use to be compatible with their own needs but not so restrictive that they will find it impossible to expand as their need for space grows. Many communities control land use through planning and zoning with a careful concern for high-technology firms' requirements. Such controls include limitations on types of uses permitted, to ensure that only clean and attractive operations are located on the site; coverage, set-backs, construction code, and maintenance restrictions, to ensure that properties are compatible in appearance; and park provisions. Streets and utilities often are developed by local government to a required standard, with access controlled to limit traffic. Lowell's attraction for Wang Laboratories was based, in part, on such initiatives. Many locally developed research parks (in which parcels are sold only to firms conducting research) can be viewed as a subclassification of this type of initiative.

Communities of each of the categories described above have engaged in these types of initiative. Such programs are not without risk. Carrying costs can be high if suitable users are not attracted, and the parks can monopolize valuable land that could be put to other productive use. Some communities ultimately have had to relax usage criteria to attract nontechnological users. Pressure for such relaxation is constant, but once undermined in this manner, the research parks may lose much of their appeal to technology-based companies.

University improvements   A number of communities have worked hard to develop engineering programs at local universities. Such initiatives have been most important in the technology installation and bootstrap communities, where local demand for such programs previously had been modest. Such initiatives have been of crucial importance in San Antonio, San Diego, Phoenix, Colorado Springs, Huntsville, and Seattle, to name the most striking examples identified in this survey. Such initiatives include efforts to create an engineering department at a university that has not had one; add graduate programs; upgrade the overall quality of the program; and/or bring faculty to the university with specializations in areas of importance to local industry. Another university-related initiative is the establishment of a research center to conduct contract research for industry.

Vocational/technical training   As a specific initiative for the purpose of attracting high-technology firms, this approach is most common in diluted centers, technology installation centers, and bootstrap communities. It can take the form of adding specific training programs required by local industry or the development of high-technology "magnet" high schools. Such initiatives often begin with an assessment of what skills are required by local industry; courses are then designed with input from those businesses most likely to hire graduates.

Incubator buildings   These are most often built in areas where the quantity of high-quality speculative space for small users is limited. Such areas include inner-city portions of diluted centers and smaller communities without a large high-technology base. Such facilities require experienced real estate management, and (as with research parks) carrying costs can be high if they are not utilized. In addition, technology-based tenants often require technical and management assistance. Similar initiatives have been undertaken by both universities and private industry.

Marketing programs   Virtually all communities conduct marketing programs to attract new industry. However, those localities with the most sophisticated programs directed at high-technology companies tend to be those that already have experienced the greatest success in attracting them. These include communities in all of the categories listed above, with the exception of the high-technology centers themselves, but the programs differ in their focus depending on the type of community involved. For example, the spillover communities are most likely to direct their efforts toward companies located in the city to which they are adjacent, while bootstrap communities primarily seek to attract labor-intensive, less technical branch operations of technology-based companies.

Key ingredients of these initiatives include the identification of specific firms to which the community would have the greatest appeal, the improvement of the community to make sure that required infrastructure or amenities are in place, and a concerted marketing effort through direct mail, telephone contacts, and personal visits to the prospect companies.

In some cases, marketing programs have been conducted without an adequate understanding of the requirements of high-technology firms or without a thorough evaluation of the community attributes that high-technology firms are likely to find of interest. This can result in missing the market or overselling the community. In such cases, the time, funds, and effort spent on marketing bring poor results.

High-technology task forces   Engaged in by many communities and states, this initiative serves to focus local attention and resources on high-technology economic development. Local task forces usually are appointed by mayors, although they are sometimes an adjunct of the chamber of commerce. They generally include representatives from industry, education, and government. They are distinct from other initiatives in that they are not designed to overcome some limitation in a community's ability to attract or retain high-technology companies. Instead, they have a designing function and, in some cases, participate in implementation. They also have a pronounced networking effect and thus are used most commonly in diluted high-technology centers, such as Chicago and Minneapolis, where such efforts are the first step in overcoming the effects of dilution.

Venture capital funds   Most of the local representatives interviewed for this study recognized the importance of venture capital to HTD, but few expressed satisfaction with their initiatives to fill this need. Planned and existing efforts included seminars or conferences for venture capital firms and local entrepreneurs, the identification of local venture capital resources, and consulting assistance in procuring venture capital. Only one community of those surveyed, Cincinnati, was seriously considering the establishment of a venture capital fund. However, OTA has identified such efforts in a few other communities.

Effective venture capital programs directed at high-technology companies presuppose a substantial number of high-technology innovations in a community each year. Without a major university or a large existing base of research-oriented firms, it is doubtful that an adequate number of innovations with commercial potential will be found in a community. The critical mass of innovations is most likely to be found in the true high-technology or diluted high-technology centers. These areas are also the ones most likely to have existing, private venture capital operations, which may explain some of the problems that other communities are having with this type of initiative.

Other initiatives   Other, less common initiatives include efforts to attract a specific company. In some cases, the contributions of a single firm to an area were viewed as being so great and as having such an impact on the future HTD of the area, that a major initiative was devoted to the specific firm. The efforts to bring Wang Laboratories' headquarters to Lowell provide the best example of such a focused marketing drive; Austin's successful campaign to attract MCC provides a more recent example.

Also, realizing that companies seeking to recruit large numbers of researchers are concerned about amenities and cultural opportunities for these workers, one community (Huntsville) developed a large civic center to house visiting orchestras and other cultural events. Several cities are considering the establishment of research institutes (private contract research organizations not directly affiliated with a university), with Cincinnati's Institute of Advanced Manufacturing Sciences being the most developed. In one diluted high-technology center, Chicago, a high-technology newsletter was felt to be an important tool for overcoming the effects of dilution.

Several initiatives are based on "partnerships" between local government and the various components of the community's educational and technological base. For example, there is usually a strong relationship between research parks (occupied by industrial research laboratories) and local universities; in many of the cases, the development of research parks has been a cooperative initiative in which the original stimulus was the university. Local vocational/technical programs, too, typically have strong ties to both state and local training programs, and many have received federal funding. Additionally, the private sector (and especially the technology-based business already located in the community) has made major contributions of time and effort to local initiatives. This is particularly true of task forces but also of programs to improve university engineering and scientific programs.

Program design and effectiveness

Sources of information   The surveyed communities got their ideas for high-technology initiatives from a variety of sources. Most local officials followed discussions of high-technology and economic development in journals, magazines, and newspapers; many also had collected reports issued by state and local governments on the subject. Additionally, there was often direct contact among the communities on high-technology issues related to economic development. For example, in several cases, public officials who were investigating the development of a research park visited successful parks in other communities. This was true in Binghamton, Chicago, Orlando, and Montgomery County, among others. The Puget Sound task force, which was seeking to improve scientific and engineering education in the Seattle area, invited the president of MIT to speak at a meeting. Information on other areas' initiatives also was collected through consulting studies, phone interviews, and letter requests.

Another important source of information on initiatives is the industrial prospects themselves. For example, public officials in San Antonio began lobbying for engineering programs in the city's state college after a major electronics company announced that it would not build a plant in the area because of the lack of continuing education opportunities for its employees. Local industry and business groups frequently exerted similar pressure for the improvement of vocational/technical programs to train skilled workers. In several cases, the state government or a statewide business organization encouraged initiatives by counties and universities to establish research parks. In Wisconsin, for example, both the state and the city of Milwaukee are participating in a joint marketing effort directed at the robotics industry. A final source of information for program design was the community's development efforts with other types of industry. Many high-technology marketing initiatives are adaptations of successful efforts used for many years by local economic development organizations. Similarly, task forces were a common mechanism used to address a wide range of community concerns long before this technique was applied to HTD.

Implementation Like information gathering, program implementation followed common patterns in most communities. The first step was usually to identify the need for something lacking in the community or the importance of a particular service to local high-technology firms or prospects. Once the need or opportunity was identified, many communities explored their resources and policy tools with consultants, local businessmen, and other knowledgeable informants. For example, in exploring potential participation of the local government or university in a research park, the community would need to know what protective convenants or tax changes would help as well as what types of firms would qualify for the park and how many jobs they would create. In launching and operating the program, communities must adapt the experiences of other communities to their own specific situation and avoid the weaknesses and pitfalls (if any) of their models.

Federal and state participation Agents of the federal government participated directly in the initiatives in several of the surveyed cities. For example, the High Technology Task Force in Chicago was chaired by the director of the Argonne National Laboratories. Significantly, the local organizations responsible for high-technology programs made frequent use of the funds and other development tools made available by the federal government. The most frequently mentioned federal programs and development tools in relation to specific initiatives in 22 surveyed communities were: Urban Development Action Grants (9), industrial development bonds (5), Economic Development Administration grants (4), Community Development Block Grants (3), Comprehensive Education and Training Act programs (2), free trade zones (2), Appalachian Regional Commission programs (2), and Small Business Administration loan programs (1).

Although none of these federal programs were designed specifically to help with high-technology development, this finding shows that they have been successfully applied to such purposes.

Major federal R&D installations frequently provided the base around which high-technology programs are built. In several cases, in fact, it was the reduction of federal support for these installations that provided the impetus for developing a local economic development program directed at high-technology companies. This was true in both Brevard County and Huntsville. Also, military bases were often cited as good sources of skilled labor for high-technology companies located in an area. This is true in such cities as San Antonio, San Diego, and Colorado Springs. In such cases, the federal government has in effect subsidized technical training for workers who subsequently feed into the local private economy.

State governments also participated in local initiatives, frequently through their control of university and vocational/technical education resources. State marketing programs also complemented those of the local communities.

Innovation v. attraction   Although most of the local representatives interviewed for this survey recognized the importance of stimulating new local companies built around innovative products, the greatest efforts were directed at attracting branch operations of large high-technology firms. This strategy pays more immediate dividends in terms of job creation, but another reason seems to be the relatively small number of communities in which a significant number of innovative new products are developed. In the true high-technology centers, there seems to be a "critical mass" for the creation of new companies, which in turn warrants the concentrated attention of venture capital firms and other development organizations. This critical mass is missing in cities with smaller technology-oriented industrial bases. At least initially, it may not be cost effective in such cities to devote local resources to initiatives aimed at entrepreneurial ventures. In time, however, the attraction of several branch plants may result in the necessary concentration of firms, technical workers, and potential entrepreneurs. Several cities reviewed for this study—including Minneapolis–St. Paul, Austin, and San Diego—are reaching the stage at which a significant number of new high-technology companies can be spawned, but they are the exception rather than the rule.

Factors affecting success

Not all of the communities investigated for this study have been equally successful in becoming high-technology centers. Given the differences in their goals and strategies, absolute criteria for success are difficult to determine and, as with state initiatives, these programs have not been subjected to rigorous comparative analysis or evaluation. As a result, measures of success are somewhat impressionistic. Nevertheless the collective experience of these 22 communities indicates that the following factors condition the effectiveness of local programs for HTD:

1. *Sustained effort,* often over a period of decades
2. *Identifying local needs and resources*
3. *Adapting to external constraints,* including climate, distance from existing high-technology centers, and other factors over which the community has no control
4. *Linkage to other, broader development efforts*
5. *Local initiative and partnership* in the initiation, implementation, and operation of the program.

Sustained local effort   Although some of the 22 communities were able to reap rapid results from their initiatives, few have developed large concentrations of high-technology establishments in a short time. A minimum of 20 years may be a realistic period for a community to develop to the stage where a significant number of local jobs can be credited to products created by local entrepreneurs or local research establishments of larger companies. This long timeframe should not be discouraging, however, since many of the "bootstrap" and "spillover" communities improved their economies quickly and significantly by attracting branch plants of technology-based companies. Huntsville, Phoenix, San Diego, Colorado Springs, Lowell, and Austin had all been working successfully for many years to attract technology-based branch operations.

Identifying needs and resources   A second factor is clear recognition of the local attributes, both strengths and weaknesses, that influence a community's ability to attract high-technology industry. In the more successful cases, such analyses of the community were conducted by local representatives or by outside consultants. With clear objectives, the community was then able to develop appropriate development strategies.

Adapting to external constraints   There are other factors over which a community has little control, such as climate, terrain, and proximity to existing high-technology centers. The successful communities recognized these external constraints and adjusted their objectives and strategies accordingly. Thus, both Colorado Springs and Austin initially focused their marketing efforts on branch plants rather than on research- or technology-intensive establishments. Over time, as these branch plants created a base of skilled labor and technical infrastructure, they have been able to attract more sophisticated operations and encourage local spinoffs.

Linkage to other efforts   The local initiatives that formed part of a broader development strategy often produced the most substantial results. Two examples of this pattern are worth reviewing. San Diego had conducted several analyses to determine the types of industry that would find the area most attractive and had targeted several specific high-technology operations like consumer electronics. The community also identified the large quantity of available land as a major asset, and most of its initiatives are based on exploiting this resource to achieve its HTD objective. In Huntsville, community leaders commissioned a detailed assessment at the time of the downturn in employment at the Redstone Arsenal, and the pool of skilled labor created by the Arsenal was recognized as a major attribute that could be marketed to technology-based firms. Other initiatives were also developed to make the community more attractive to such operations, including the creation of a research park and the contruction of the community center. Huntsville conducts periodic reassessments to monitor changes in local conditions that would warrant shifts in this strategy.

Local initiative and partnership   Finally, it is worth noting that in the successful communities, most of the effort has been initiated and implemented locally. Some communities received substantial help from state governments in developing university resources and complementing the local marketing program. Others have used funding and a number of development tools made possible by the federal government. But in most cases, the objectives and strategies were developed locally, and local representatives had a major part in design and implementation of the programs. In addition, cooperation or "partnership" with local entrepreneurs and business groups plays an important role in successful programs, since the public and private sectors are far less distinct at the local level.

Local policy tools   Local governments have at their disposal a wide range of policy tools that have been used to provide incentives for the necessary private sector participation.[1] Some, like zoning bonuses or minority hiring quotas, encourage or require private initiative; others, like administrative reform, tax relief, or infrastructure improvements, remove barriers to private initiative. The effectiveness of some of these tools may be constrained by the policies and regulations of state or federal government; in such cases, public and private leaders at the local level often have joined forces to overcome these constraints. Policy tools that are in the control of local government include the following:

1. *Provision of public services,* including improved public safety, education system reforms, and recreational or cultural programs
2. *Provision of public facilities,* such as improvements to water, sewer, and road systems, improved mass transit, and public parks
3. *Tax policies,* such as relief from property tax or incentives for inner-city location, as well as lower overall tax rates
4. *Regulatory policies,* including changes in zoning or building codes that will encourage rehabilitation
5. *Administrative reforms,* such as improved financial practices, one-stop permitting, or streamlined licensing and inspection systems
6. *Public advocacy,* including public recognition for private initiatives and support for business interests in state legislatures.

1. Tom Chmura, et al., *Redefining Partnership—Developing Public/ Private Approaches to Community Problem Solving: A Guide for Local Officials* (Menlo Park, Calif.: SRI International, January 1982), p. 16; see also SRI International, *Developing Public/Private Approaches to Community Problem Solving,* Management Information Service Report, International City Management Association, vol. 14, No. 7, July 1982, pp. 5-6, 17.

PART 4

Successful Local Economic Development Efforts

No Lost Causes: Salvaging Neighborhood Shopping Districts

Lawrence Hall, Robert H. Lurcott,
Karen LaFrance, Michael A. Dobbins

New Haven: private money first

Editor's note: This section was prepared by Lawrence Hall, Neighborhood Assistance Coordinator, Office of Housing and Neighborhood Development, New Haven, Connecticut.

The premise of New Haven's commercial revitalization program is simple: Public investment is tied to private performance. The city makes public improvements only in those areas where merchants are ready to commit themselves to major revitalization efforts. In other words, the city helps those who help themselves.

It works this way. Merchants in a neighborhood express interest in being designated a neighborhood commercial revitalization district. A merchants' association is formed, and over half of the merchants or property owners in the district agree, in writing, to renovate their buildings. The extent of renovation required depends on individual circumstances; however, the commitment must be specific in terms of the work being done and the costs. The association then identifies development goals and objectives and establishes a design review committee, composed of merchants, property owners, and city staff, to approve rehabilitation designs.

After designation, each owner is eligible for up to $15,000 in city matching grants. The Office of Economic Development helps with loan packaging and technical assistance.

When half of the buildings have been renovated, the district becomes eligible for public improvements and the city's "self-help grants," available to support such activities as advertising campaigns, festivals, and market studies. (The city puts up $1 for every $2 expended by the neighborhood group.) The two-year time limit on the self-help grants is an incentive to quick action.

The city negotiates the public improvements—street trees, sidewalks, parking lots, and so on—with the design review committee.

Since June 1980 when the first city grants were issued, some $500,000 in rehabilitation grants and $1 million in public improvements have leveraged about $5 million in private investment in two commercial areas.

One of those areas is Lower Whalley Avenue, the region's traditional auto row. By the mid-1970s, the number of dealerships had dwindled to five—down from 12 in 1960. Dealers who left cited as their reasons obsolete facilities and fear of crime. Other businesses followed, although there are still a substantial number of muffler, auto glass, and body shops. In 1977, a Whalley Avenue Association was formed and a director hired.

In 1979, Biagio DiLieto, campaigning for his first term as New Haven's mayor from an office on Whalley Avenue, made the condition of the street an issue. After his election, he called for a revitalization program, emphasizing the need for cooperation among merchants, property owners, and the city.

The results so far have been encouraging: the $1 million renovation of a vacant auto dealership into Storer Cable Television's regional headquarters; the renovation of three auto dealerships and several related businesses; the construction of two new fast food franchises; and several new businesses. Now that a majority of the storefronts have been renovated, the city is installing new sidewalks, bus stops, and grass planter strips along the curbs.

The impressive strength of the private sector resurgence on Whalley Avenue has offset some of the early problems, including inadequate front-end planning and a lack of design criteria. The design shortcomings have given a few of the early renovations an uneven quality. And confusion about district boundaries created uncertainty among merchants about who was eligible for facade grants. The city has developed stricter guidelines for other districts.

The Whalley Avenue Association has an ambitious agenda for 1983. It plans to publish a parking locator map, put up street banners, and promote special sales events. The association has also prepared a proposal for a special services district—a vehicle for imposing a surtax on area businesses to fund the activities of the association.

New Haven's program has been just as effective in a very different type of area, Upper State Street, a turn-of-the-century neighborhood whose population includes longtime Polish and Italian residents, black and Hispanic newcomers, Yale students and staff, and downtown workers attracted by the reasonable rents and convenient location. A few years ago, Upper State Street was deteriorating, and many of its merchants had fled to the suburbs.

Today, the neighborhood has a new, more positive image of itself, in part because of the efforts of the Upper State Street Association, which includes property owners and merchants, longtime residents and young professionals (particularly architects). The group originally lacked political sophistication, but it has attracted support because of its vitality.

Renovation has transformed the neighborhood. Several new businesses have opened—a pastry shop, two new restaurants, and two clothing stores. There will be some $500,000 in new townhouse development with potential ground-floor office space on a city-owned site and gut rehab of several residential-commerical buildings. The city is currently building a parking lot, replacing crumbling sidewalks and curbs, and adding a strip of concrete pavers, street trees, and benches along the curb.

The Upper State Street program has affected the entire community. Planning for the area has emphasized the integration of housing and commercial activity, and the participation on the design review committee of architects who live in the neighborhood has resulted in high-quality renovations.

The next step for Upper State Street is to work on creating a Main Street atmosphere through promotions, festivals, and other people-drawing activities. Also, the Upper State Street Association intends to file an application for national historic district status. If it's approved, local property owners will be able to take advantage of federal tax credits.

Pittsburgh: market studies

Editor's note: This section was prepared by Robert H. Lurcott, Planning Director, and Karen LaFrance, Senior Planner, Pittsburgh, Pennsylvania.

It has been nearly 10 years since the Pittsburgh planning department first took on some of the city's most decayed neighborhood commercial districts. In that time, we have learned much that can be applied elsewhere. The city's approach in the early 1970s was a physical one. It offered relatively low-interest loans for facade renovation, provided new parking lots, and made various street improvements.

Clearly, that hasn't been enough. In the last several years, the city has changed the course of its commercial revitalization program, expanding some aspects and modifying others. Changes grew out of market studies in two business districts—East Liberty and Hazelwood; suggestions from the National Development Council (the nonprofit group associated with economic development guru John Sower); an evaluation of the city's Neighborhood Commercial Loan Program; and heightened public demand for assistance.

The planning department has added a staff position for a neighborhood commercial revitalization coordinator. In addition, the city's capital budget now includes funds for market studies and for assisting small businesses with promotion and coordination. An interagency committee, chaired by a mayoral assistant and including the heads of the planning department and urban redevelopment authority, was set up as a clearinghouse for city assistance. The planning department is responsible for market evaluation and community liaison, and the urban redevelopment authority administers the commercial loan program.

The city has funded market studies in nine areas. Shoppers, merchants, and residents in all of them voiced similar complaints about "unappealing stores" and "dirty conditions." However, the areas differed in significant ways and required different approaches to revitalization, as these examples show.

East Liberty, an early focus of attention, has, in effect, become the city's commercial revitalization laboratory. This East End neighborhood includes a 450,000-square-foot shopping district, which underwent extensive urban renewal in the 1960s. Part of the area was closed to traffic. By the late 1970s, merchants were expressing dissatisfaction with traffic patterns and parking, the image of the district as a high crime area had worsened, and sales were declining.

The market study, completed in 1978, concluded that East Liberty no longer served its traditional regional market. Rather, it had become a convenience center for the surrounding neighborhood. The study noted that shop owners were generally older and unwilling to change merchandising practices to capture a younger, fashion-conscious (although not very affluent) market.

The consultants suggested that the mall be reopened to auto traffic, the police presence increased, and merchandising practices updated. The city has spent nearly $600,000 in community development funds to reopen the mall and to support merchandising and promotion programs.

The city's attempt to fund activities other than physical improvements was the most promising aspect of the new program. At the planning department's request, the East Liberty Chamber of Commerce set up a development corporation, East Liberty Development, Inc. (ELDI), to receive community development funds for promotion. Last year, ELDI became a full-fledged development entity with its own staff and financial support from major banks and corporations, social service agencies, and neighborhood churches. The city is committed to contributing $50,000 in community development funds over the next two years to help ELDI rehabilitate vacant buildings and to improve East Liberty's image through a public relations campaign.

In the second year, ELDI and the city will consider setting up a special tax assessment district to raise administrative and promotional funds in the future.

In the much smaller (90,000 square feet) Second Avenue business district in the Hazelwood neighborhood, two blocks were cleared in the early 1970s for a retail mini-mall. The neighborhood's population continued to decline, however, and its image worsened. In the late 1970s, part of the mini-mall site was used for subsidized housing for the elderly.

In 1979, a planning department market analysis showed that the area could support only a modest number of convenience shops and some auto supply stores. The $266,700 left over from a state renewal project allocation could not solve all the district's problems. Local merchants and the city agreed on a limited program of public improvements, including new sidewalks and brick ramps for the handicapped. Plans are under way now to paint the facades and boarded-up windows of vacant buildings.

A market study of the 12-block-long Penn Avenue business district in the Bloomfield-Garfield neighborhood was the key to putting that area's program on a realistic basis. In response to a community organization's request for funds, the city asked for an evaluation by an outside consultant to determine how much revitalization could reasonably be expected. The consultant said the market area could no longer support a large business district (189,000 square feet retail and 100,000 square feet light industrial and commercial, with a vacancy rate of almost 20 percent) and recommended consolidation.

The city has since paid for a "district coordinator," who is concentrating on a three-block area near the community organization's storefront office. In a year and a half, the coordinator has had modest success in encouraging facade rehab, starting up small businesses, and negotiating the purchase of vacant buildings for rehab.

In the small (80,000 square feet), troubled, commercial core of Homewood, a large, predominantly black neighborhood, the market study led to a change in emphasis in a state-funded renewal project. Once again, consolidation was recommended and is actually being implemented. The anchors for the consolidation are a new fast food outlet and a new community college branch. A community planner assigned to the neighborhood has organized a community development corporation, which will undertake security and promotion programs.

A market study also can help show that a business district no longer needs city assistance. That was the case with Western Avenue, three blocks (131,000 square feet) of mixed retail and residential uses in the newly gentrified Allegheny West neighborhood. This district contains both boutiques and convenience stores, the latter important to lower income residents of adjacent neighborhoods. The study concluded that more boutiques were likely to locate in the district without city assistance and without displacing convenience stores.

On East Ohio Street (141,000 square feet), an outside consultant recommended a promotion and store recruitment campaign to build on the district's current market strength as a collection of specialty stores.

Building on what it has learned, Pittsburgh has made several changes in its commercial district programs:

1. The city's Neighborhood Commercial Loan Program has been redirected from building rehabilitation to storefront facade rehabilitation targeted to commercially zoned properties in designated commercial districts. To complement this loan program, the urban development authority is putting in place a new, tax-exempt, long-term, rehabilitation financing program.

    Separate funding support continues for market studies, business development, and staff support for business organizations in designated areas.

2. A major effort is being made to ensure long-term participation by businesses in commercial districts. Public improvements will now be undertaken only in those areas where a business organization agrees to a maintenance code enforcement program.

3. The city is encouraging business districts to make use of special tax assessments (in areas where a substantial majority of property owners agree) to fund promotional efforts and pay for administrative staff.

Birmingham: design is the key

Editor's note: This section was prepared by Michael A. Dobbins, Architect, Department of Community Development, Birmingham, Alabama.

Five years ago, the commercial district of the North Birmingham neighborhood was in terrible shape, with many vacancies, severe physical deterioration, and sagging morale. Today, things are far different—the result of positive intervention by the city, local merchants, and investors. What happened in North Birmingham illustrates in a dramatic way the effectiveness of the planning process—and especially of a dogged commitment by both public and private partners to see a program through.

Birmingham has a tradition of strong neighborhoods (all organized into an elaborate participatory structure and all receiving a set allocation of the city's revenue sharing funds); and both mayor Richard Arrington, Jr., and his predecessor, David Vann, have viewed neighborhood development as a central part of their programs. In 1976, Mayor Vann set up 12 economic revitalization committees, composed of neighborhood business leaders, property owners, and officers of neighborhood associations.

North Birmingham was one of the first neighborhoods to receive attention. About two miles north of the downtown and ringed by heavy industry, this mile-square, working class neighborhood had shifted from 90 percent white in 1970 to 90 percent black by 1978. Its commercial center once served a broad community of about two-and-a-half square miles as well as the rural mining areas north of the city line.

Before World War II, the entire north rim of Birmingham was like a series of mill towns, each with its own shopping area. After the war, the suburbs captured the population growth, the new shopping malls—and the customers. Shop vacancies in North Birmingham increased steadily. The economic revitalization committee, which began meeting in 1976, provided a forum in which neighborhood merchants could discuss the problems and the options available. In short, a planning process was launched.

The lessons learned from that experience (summarized in the accompanying box) have provided the basis for increasingly efficient and effective programs in other Birmingham neighborhoods.

One of the first steps was to invite the American Institute of Architects to send in a Rural/Urban Design Assistance Team for an intense, multidisciplinary examination of North Birmingham and two other neighborhood commercial centers. The R/UDAT team showed in graphic form how North Birmingham could look. That, in turn, sparked the imagination of some of the neighborhood merchants.

In June 1977, the city commissioned two consultants, National Urban Development Services, Inc., of Washington (now Urban Development Services) and Kidd, Wheeler, and Plosser of Birmingham (now Kidd, Plosser, and Sprague) to conduct a detailed planning study.

The study produced these findings:

1.   That the North Birmingham business district could no longer sustain the amount of commercial space it could during its heyday as a regional center; consolidation from approximately 15 blocks to about six would provide the best chance of retaining existing businesses and avoiding scattered vacancies.
2.   That a substantial increase in readily accessible parking was needed.

3. That some of the seriously deteriorated storefronts would have to be removed and the rest substantially rehabilitated.
4. That major, new, private investment in the area was essential.
5. That the merchants, property owners, and neighborhood residents would have to assume more of a leadership role in the revitalization effort.

A plan based on these principles was approved by the city and the neighborhood merchants in early 1979.

The plan focused on several core blocks on which the redevelopment efforts should be concentrated. Certain old buildings were identified for rehabilitation. Other sites were identified for redevelopment. A landscaped "parking mall" was proposed to establish a link between the main traffic-carrying street (26th Street) and the shopping street (27th Street). New landscaping was proposed for 27th Street. The plan also proposed that several commercial properties outside the new core commercial area be converted to housing.

What we learned

In New Haven
• Front-end planning is crucial to link neighborhood residential and commercial needs in a common strategy and to resolve boundary issues.
• Creating a design committee allows merchants to exercise aesthetic control and shifts responsibility away from the city. It is essential, however, that the city provide competent technical assistance to the committee.
• Program deadlines (like our two-year limit on facade improvements) motivate the private sector.
• Instead of attempting to dictate market decisions, a commercial revitalization program should attempt to create a climate of confidence in which the market can reestablish itself.
• Long-term success depends on a permanent organization and a continuing source of revenue for promotion and maintenance.

In Pittsburgh
• Study the market carefully, evaluate the commercial district's economic future, and make a realistic assessment of its potential. A market study can ferret out specific opportunities that the private market may have missed. For, despite the middle-class shift to the suburbs, city households are still a substantial source of shopping dollars. A market study can be particularly useful in deciding which areas may not have a significant future as retailing centers. In such areas, the appropriate treatment may not be "commercial revitalization" as we generally view it.

New construction was to include housing, expansion of an existing medical clinic, and a new, 25,000-square-foot supermarket. As called for in the contract, the consultants became involved in the first steps of implementation, including early negotiations for the city's first Urban Development Action Grant. The UDAG application brought three private sector partners together: a hospital, a supermarket firm, and a developer of Section 8 housing for the elderly. The city's role was to assemble the land and relocate existing businesses and residents and (as described below) to work with storeowners on a facade improvement program. Kidd, Wheeler, and Plosser was commissioned to prepare contract documents for the recommended public improvements.

The UDAG partnership proved to be unstable. By the time construction started, two of the original partners had been replaced and the third had significantly altered its plans. All the changes required amendments in the application and caused delays and rearrangement of financing agreements.

But despite the problems, the city's decision to inject itself into

---

• The community and the city must agree on the objectives of the revitalization effort and the nature of the city's assistance. That means that there must be an effective community organization. Ideally, retailers should participate, especially in the market study phase.
• Private reinvestment must encompass more than facade and public space improvements. Our evaluation showed that even districts whose merchants were heavily involved in the city's facade rehab program continued to suffer from market and image problems. Since commercial districts are in competition with modern shopping malls, merchants must know their market as intimately as mall managers know theirs. They must invest in their businesses, modernize their retailing practices and collectively upgrade their promotion and marketing efforts.
• Target public assistance where it will have the most impact, and tailor it to the needs of specific districts.

In Birmingham
• The success of a program depends on the inclusion of all sides in the planning process—merchants, property owners, investors, neighborhood leaders, and city staff.
• A mandatory rehabilitation program will produce physical changes and encourage investment. In North Birmingham, $25,000 of city rebate money leveraged $135,000 in private investment.
• UDAGs should be structured as simply as possible. Avoid multiparty agreements where each party's participation is contingent on all the others'.
• As a program proves its effectiveness, it becomes easier to extend it to other areas and to get the private sector to chip in.

neighborhood business revitalization appears to be justified. The investment of public dollars (the $947,878 UDAG, $1,418,257 in CDBG funds, $147,851 in revenue sharing, and $697,826 in city bonds) leveraged a $9 million private investment—yielding 125 new housing units, the clinic, the supermarket, 60 new jobs, and 30 rehabilitated storefronts. The program did what it promised. It made more goods and services available to the community, added jobs, and built links between neighborhood and business leaders. The city's interest was to improve the tax base, which it did. The increased tax take is estimated at $120,000 a year.

An unusual aspect of Birmingham's program is its mandatory storefront rehabilitation, coupled with a rebate to property owners and merchants who comply. So far, $25,000 in city rebate money has leveraged $135,000 worth of private improvements, covering 32 storefronts. Each rebate was approved by the design review committee established by the city council as part of the 1979 ordinance.

The mandatory rehabilitation program was modeled after a program that began in Baltimore in 1970. Since Birmingham adopted its version in 1979, a dozen or so cities have followed suit.

As the commercial revitalization program has been extended to other neighborhoods, the initial skepticism and resistance has gradually given way to hope and even a modest backlog in demand on the city for implementation. In one area, neighborhood merchants are even pushing to make the mandatory storefront rehab requirement applicable to a larger area than originally proposed.

This change in attitude has enabled the city to establish a few modest threshhold requirements and to expect a higher leverage rate. The program has also shown a kind of countercyclical success —proving effective at a time when the New Federalism has scaled down the availability of public funds. Hard times seem to produce recognition of the reality that cooperation and unity of purpose are in the best interest of everyone involved.

Reforming Zoning Regulations to Encourage Economic Development

Bruce W. McClendon

Over the years, zoning has been a subject of major local controversy in Beaumont [Texas] (pop. 118,000).

The city adopted its first comprehensive zoning ordinance in 1948 and repealed it the same year when it was recalled by special election.

In 1955 a compromise zoning ordinance was adopted with the support of the local development community. Three years later a national consulting firm was hired to prepare a comprehensive plan and to update the zoning ordinance. The consulting firm concluded that the 1955 ordinance was "very defective" and recommended adoption of a completely new ordinance.

Subsequently, a new zoning ordinance which reflected the consultant's recommendations was prepared and submitted to the city council for adoption. However, this ordinance was rejected by the council and the original 1955 ordinance was left basically unchanged until the present time.

Justification for change

Since 1960 the population growth of Beaumont has been minimal despite glowing predictions to the contrary. Over time, regulatory reform became recognized as an important contributing factor for economic development. It was generally agreed that revising and updating the zoning ordinance was necessary to ensure that the community remain competitive with other development markets, while also providing local residents and developers with the oppor-

Reprinted with permission from the August 1982 issue of *Texas Town & City*, published by the Texas Municipal League.

tunity to take advantage of more efficient or economical types of development.

A review and evaluation of the Beaumont zoning ordinance convinced the city planning staff that its many inadequacies were seriously discouraging and restricting local economic development. The planning staff classified over 40 major deficiencies in the zoning ordinance into the following general categories:

1. Defects in the original ordinance
2. Deficiencies created by improper or lax administration and subsequent amendments to the original ordinance which were inconsistent, conflicting, or ambiguous
3. Inconsistency with state statutes or judicial decisions
4. Failure to reflect current public opinion and prevailing community values and
5. Failure to reflect current zoning concepts and innovative development practices.

The list of deficiencies ranged from poor organization and lack of clarity to exclusionary zoning practices and outright conflicts with state enabling legislation. Where limited provisions had been made for such innovative development techniques as cluster housing, the regulations were overly restrictive and time consuming, and they unnecessarily hampered opportunities for flexible creative developments.

The deficiencies in the zoning ordinance were having an obvious negative impact on local economic development. New types of development were being discouraged and, in many instances, development costs were being inflated by unnecessary and excessive regulation. For example, the minimum lot sizes for single-family residential development were larger than necessary, which contributed to making the cost of housing in Beaumont higher than the regional average.

Many new developments and uses were not provided for in the list of permitted uses. This meant that the zoning officer could not always immediately respond to informational requests from potential developers. Often the staff had to confer with the legal department or undertake analytical studies to determine whether a proposed use would be permitted in a particular zoning district.

Compounding this problem was the fact that no list of permitted uses existed for the heavy industrial district and each and every proposed heavy industrial use had to be approved by the board of adjustment. The uncertainty and delay caused by this situation had an adverse effect on the city's ability to compete for industrial prospects.

Interestingly enough, while the ordinance was unnecessarily hampering development, the lack of certain minimum regulations to protect existing single-family development from the consequences of other forms of development was making it increasingly difficult to obtain public support and council approval for rezoning. Failure to require any side or rear yard setbacks or any type of screening for commercial and industrial development resulted in increased residential incompatibility and opposition to development.

The deficient list of permitted uses in the numerous multi-family and commercial districts also increased rezoning difficulties. The permitted uses in the various districts had not been prepared according to related areas of similarity, compatibility, external effects, or functional interrelationships. As a result, many rezoning requests were being denied even though the city council, planning commission, and adjacent property owners were in support of the applicant's intended use for the property.

Applications were denied because the requested zoning district also permitted uses which would have been harmful to the neighborhood. The failure to have more functionally compatible districts and the inability to ensure development compatibility with a specific use permit had led to rejection of development proposals ranging from shopping centers to beauty shops.

The increasing public opposition to rezoning and the surge in citizen complaints about new developments that were taking place, together with a growing desire to remain competitive and encourage more economical and efficient development opportunities, all combined to provide the consensus which was needed to support the regulatory reform process.

The process

The revision and updating of Beaumont's zoning ordinance took place over a two-year period from 1979 to 1981 and involved six public hearings, 38 workshops, three public forums, and numerous subcommittee meetings.

The local development community was an active, although sometimes reluctant, participant in the process. After initially supporting the reform process, the local builders' association at one point attempted to stop the process, and even formed a political action committee for the purpose of increasing their influence with local elected officials.

The opposition of many local developers to changing the ordinance was based on the following factors:

1. Distrust of the local planning staff
2. Misunderstanding of the flexibility and negotiation concept in zoning
3. Opposition from developers who had drafted the 1955 ordinance

4. Opposition to any type of zoning
5. Reluctance to trust the judgment of the elected officials who would be making the final decision
6. Belief that the members of the planning commission were not familiar with local development practices and problems
7. Satisfaction with the current regulations and
8. General fear of change.

Despite opposition from the development community, the planning commission and city council continued their efforts to revise the ordinance. Both bodies remained convinced that the final product would ultimately have the acceptance and support of the development community.

The new draft ordinance, which had been prepared by the city planning staff, was continuously revised as a result of input from the various hearings and workshops. The spirit of cooperation and compromise which local planners, the planning commission, and the city council exhibited during the review process was reflected in the ordinance that was finally adopted. Today there is almost unanimous agreement that the new zoning ordinance will be a positive stimulus to economic development.

Perhaps the area of greatest disappointment in the reform process was the lack of general public interest and participation. Despite newspaper coverage and numerous public hearings, workshops and forums, and even written notification to every property-owner in the city, actual participation was obtained only from special interest groups and a handful of residents. The issues which were raised during the revision process were controversial and substantive, yet general public interest was almost nonexistent. Under these circumstances, the planning staff and the planning commission had to be aggressive in providing leadership for the regulatory changes needed to protect the welfare of the general public.

The product

The following is a generalized description of the significant changes which were made in the ordinance in the interest of stimulating economic growth and development.

Ordinance simplification As mentioned earlier, the original ordinance had often been a serious impediment to development. In general, confusing complexity in any zoning ordinance can produce regulatory duplication, hinder citizen participation in the decision making process, discourage innovations, lead to uncoordinated decisions, and delay development. Everybody is hurt by the inefficiency resulting from regulatory complexity—the consumer, the developer, the governmental decision-maker, environmental interest groups, and the general public.

Unlike its predecessor, the new ordinance is logically organized and indexed, and charts and tables were substituted for written narrative in order to reduce the length of the regulations and assist in developing an understanding of the ordinance.

For example, written regulations controlling minimum lot area, width, depth, yard, and height regulations were combined into a simplified chart and placed in a special section of the ordinance. In addition, diagrams and graphic illustrations were included in the appendix of the ordinance to help clarify the meaning of individual regulatory provisions and the specialized definitions in the ordinance.

Additionally, separate lists of permitted uses for each district were combined into a single chart based on the coding system in the U.S. Department of Commerce's *Standard Industrial Classification (SIC) Manual*. Reference to the SIC manual made it possible to reduce the length of the zoning ordinance while also making it more comprehensive and less subject to misinterpretation.

The regulations governing cluster housing were reduced from eight pages to three pages and most of the minimum design standards were eliminated. In addition, the specific use permit requirement was removed and cluster housing was listed as a permitted use in any residential zoning district, with maximum density being determined by a function of the underlying zoning district classification.

The unnecessary profusion of zoning district classifications was corrected by combining two single-family districts into one district and by combining the three existing commercial districts into a single unified commercial district.

Too many districts with trivial distinctions had over-complicated the original ordinance and created the need for frequent zone changes. At the same time, additional zoning districts were created for district developments such as the central business district, the port district, and office parks.

Cumulative zoning provisions were removed from many of the zoning districts. This was done to reduce potential opposition to the excessively large lists of permitted uses in the higher zoning districts and to protect prime industrial land from residential development.

In addition, the list of permitted uses was revised and based on functional relationships in order to be consistent with the stated purpose and intent of each district. Provisions for specific use permits were added so that compatibility requirements could be imposed upon those uses which were functionally related to other uses in the district but which were not always compatible.

Flexibility and innovation   The city planning staff and many local developers believed the existing zoning ordinance was unnecessarily rigid, antiquated in its reliance on traditional development practices, and lacked the framework needed for innovation and experimentation. To correct this situation, regulations which limited each lot to only one main building were removed and provisions for planned unit development (PUD), the zero lot line concept, performance standards, incentive zoning, and shopping center districts were added to the ordinance.

Development opportunities in most of the existing zoning districts were expanded by adding new, more intense uses to the list of permitted uses based on a specific use permit approval process. This provision was added because the opposition to many rezoning requests was often based on the expanded list of uses which a higher district would permit and not on specific objections to the actual proposed use of the property.

Landscaping bonus   Because of increased interest and desire to improve the physical appearance of the community, optional landscaping regulations were placed in the ordinance to encourage expanded landscaping while also compensating for additional development costs. In return for requiring a 10-foot landscaped strip in front yards, the minimum front yard setback was reduced from 25 feet to 15 feet.

While a 10-foot landscaped buffer strip was required between commercial, industrial, or multifamily developments and single-family districts, the new ordinance includes a substantial density bonus based on the lineal footage of the buffer strip that could amount to a 25 percent increase in density for multifamily development. Also, the new ordinance permits the area devoted to landscaping of off-street parking areas to be deducted from the total minimum off-street parking area requirements.

Regulatory reductions   All of the regulations in the pre-existing zoning ordinance were closely reviewed to ensure that they were not in excess of the minimum level of regulation necessary to protect the welfare of the general public. The following changes to the ordinance were made as a result of such review:

1. Off-street parking requirements for shopping centers were reduced by 25 percent
2. All remaining off-street parking space and design standards were lowered by various amounts and provisions were made for 25 percent of the parking spaces to be reduced to accommodate compact cars
3. Off-street parking requirements were eliminated in the central business district
4. Minimum lot area requirements in single-family residential districts were reduced between 20 and 55 percent

5. The minimum rear yard in multi-family and commercial districts was lowered from 25 feet to 10 percent of the lot depth for existing lots of record
6. Minimum residential front yard setbacks on cul-de-sacs were reduced to 15 feet
7. Powers of the board of adjustment to grant variances and exceptions were expanded and
8. The application procedure for a specific use permit was simplified and the amount and cost of required supporting information was reduced.

Cutting regulatory delay

Regulatory reform saves both time and money. When the development process is delayed, it can result in additional development costs which ultimately must be paid by the consumer, can lead to the abandonment of current proposed projects which are no longer economically feasible, and can seriously discourage future developments from locating in the community.

In the past, the city was able to process all rezoning applications in a maximum time of four to five weeks. In order to reduce rezoning processing time, the city is considering instituting special joint planning commission and city council public hearings and having the city council vote on the zoning request on the day immediately following the hearing at a regular council meeting. This will result in reducing maximum rezoning processing time to three to four weeks.

The planning commission recently formed a "Joint City Development Committee" to increase the impact of the local development community on the regulatory reform process. The committee has been charged with the following duties and responsibilities:

1. Provide guidance in streamlining all zoning and permitting processes
2. Analyze and provide recommendations on all proposed land use regulations
3. Provide special training programs on private sector development to the planning commission
4. Investigate and provide solutions to problems individual developers have encountered and
5. Provide guidance on the use of public resources to encourage private development.

Conclusion

Regulatory reform is a necessary and vital component of Beaumont's economic development strategy. In the pro-development environment which exists in Texas, constant updating of all regulations is necessary to ensure that a community not only remains competitive with other development markets but also permits and encourages economical and innovative development practices that benefit the ultimate consumer.

Not all of the changes which were made in the city's zoning ordinance resulted in reduced development costs. Some changes, in fact, will increase development costs: examples include the establishment of setbacks in commercial and industrial zoning districts, height regulations in residential zones, 10-foot buffer strips, noise performance standards, and off-street loading regulations.

But these additional development expenses were modest in impact, and were considered necessary to maintain minimum residential protection levels.

Most of the changes which increased developmental costs were made in direct response to growing public opposition to zoning changes, and were undertaken with the goal of gaining future public acceptance of a more aggressive rezoning policy.

The competitive nature of economic development no longer allows the luxury of allowing regulations to go unreviewed for any great length of time. Regulatory reform must be accepted as an integral and active part of any local economic development program.

Bloomfield, Connecticut: Helping Plants Grow Better

Cheryl A. Farr

Bloomfield at a glance

In Bloomfield, Connecticut, business development has been a high priority for elected officials and town staff for several decades. Over the years, concern focused on encouraging new business to come to Bloomfield. In the early 1970s, a survey by the Greater Hartford Chamber of Commerce helped Bloomfield's leaders recognize that they had been neglecting the expansion needs and day-to-day needs of their current industries.

Based on the survey results and the concerns raised by other actors in the development process, Bloomfield streamlined its permit process by hiring an expediter to provide "one-stop shopping" for development permits. Second, Bloomfield improved the provision of public services by assigning the role of ombudsman to the assistant town manager. Third, Bloomfield drew on the expertise of the private sector by reorganizing the Economic Development Commission, an appointed committee responsible for industrial promotion activities.

Bloomfield's town manager, Cliff Vermilya, credits the program's success largely to placing the program within his own office, which results in a well controlled, well coordinated and highly visible program. The underlying theme of the program is cooperation with the private sector. Bloomfield does not "give away the store" by offering tax breaks or questionable zoning modifications; they simply show, day-to-day, that the community is receptive to business development. The quarterly economic development newsletter's title neatly summarizes the message: *Plants Grow Better in Bloomfield.*

Reprinted with permission from *Economic Development: Building a Strategy* (Washington, D.C.: International City Management Association, 1981).

Community profile

Bloomfield, Connecticut, was incorporated in 1835 and has a population of roughly 21,000. Bloomfield prides itself on its racial, social, religious, and economic diversity; it is a community where integration works. Located in central Connecticut, its economy is strongly influenced by its proximity to Hartford as well as its accessibility by rail, interstate highways, and air to the major markets of the Northeast.

Bloomfield's history reveals a long tradition of local government awareness of its citizens' future needs. It created a town plan commission in 1917 and was the first town in Connecticut to develop a comprehensive plan. Bloomfield adopted the council-manager form of government in 1945; its system provides for nine council members elected at large who choose one of their number as mayor. An Industrial Development Commission was created soon afterwards to encourage industry to locate in Bloomfield. The post-war housing boom of the 1940s stimulated residential development to the extent that less than 10 percent of assessed properties were industrial or commercial. Concern over the resulting property tax burden on residents led council members to advocate industrial and commercial growth. At the time, Bloomfield was the only suburban Hartford community actively wooing businesses that were leaving the city or developing suburban branches. The community's pro-business attitude was well received. The Industrial Development Commission's efforts enabled elected officials to meet their goal: 50 percent of Bloomfield's tax revenues were derived from income-producing properties by the late 1950s.

During the 1960s, Bloomfield's energies were diverted from concern over industrial growth to the needs of the commercial sector. The central business district was a hodge-podge of dilapidated mixed-use buildings. Over the next several years, a proposal for urban renewal funding was developed, accepted by HUD, and approved by voters. Site clearance took place, and the old central business district was replaced by a low-profile commerical and office space mall linked by an expanded town green to the town hall, senior citizens' housing, and a new public library. The result was a strengthened commerical sector and a lovely, colonial style center which has become a source of civic pride.

Goals and strategies

As the renewal project came to a close in 1973, Bloomfield once again turned its attention toward industrial development. In the early 1970s, the town's staff and elected officials reconsidered both the goals and the procedures affecting Bloomfield's industrial development.

The town council, town manager, and Town Plan and Zoning

Commission informally discussed the procedural issue. As in many communities, environmental considerations had increased development regulation and complaints, and problems had resulted from the increasingly complicated procedures and review processes. During this period, the Greater Hartford Chamber of Commerce surveyed the economic climate of area communities. Looking at the survey results, and subsequent town action, is revealing.

An independent survey   The eight questions in the Chamber of Commerce survey were designed to elicit specific comments about the business climate of local communities, and the results of the survey proved both surprising and significant. The responses showed that one-third of Bloomfield companies interviewed were unhappy with the community's trash removal system. Equally interesting was the discovery that the respondents (29 of the 32 Bloomfield companies with more than 25 employees) projected their short-term expansion needs would *double* the current industrial sector's size and expand the labor force by 20 percent. However, almost half of the companies interviewed said that they planned to expand outside of Bloomfield. Town officials recognized that a business-residential tax base balance could be maintained only if the proposed expansion were to take place within the town.

GHCC's report emphasized that the retention of existing industries (and their projected growth) would be instrumental in strengthening central Connecticut's economic climate. Bloomfield took this message to heart and gave high priority to making local government more responsive to the problems and needs of existing industries.

The major complaint that Bloomfield's manufacturers had made was that they were unhappy with the requirement that they make private arrangements for trash removal. The town council voted to include industries in the community's weekly trash removal system. The rationale for the decision was that such enterprises pay taxes covering services they do not utilize (like schools), and therefore should be entitled to services such as trash removal, although businesses generate more waste than individual households.

Three program elements   The remaining comments from industrialists focused on zoning and touched on service issues including sewers, police, fire, and recreation. The town manager reviewed these comments in light of his earlier discussions with elected and appointed officials, and presented his recommendations to the town council and the Town Plan and Zoning Commission. The decision was made to implement his proposal to create a three-faceted program aimed at streamlining the permit process, improving the provision of public services to industry, and reactivating Bloomfield's industrial attraction program.

Implementation: staffing for economic development

The expertise of the economic development staff is probably the single most important determinant of the program's activities, as well as its success. Bloomfield focuses on traditional community roles in business development (the provision of public services and the development permit process) and marketing city-owned industrial land through an advisory committee composed of local bankers, realtors, and developers. The staff that town manager Vermilya hired for the economic development program is well suited to its duties.

Ombudsman   The town's assistant manager is the ombudsman in Bloomfield's business development program. He visits industries and most major commercial enterprises in Bloomfield at least once every two years. The purpose of his visits is to respond to the problems and needs of local industries, but more importantly to maintain the business community's awareness that he is there to help if problems arise. He works closely with businesses interested in moving to Bloomfield, showing them industrial sites and offering a tour of the community. Knowledgeable about the town and the town staff, the ombudsman is effective and well accepted by the private sector.

Expediter   The town's permit process expediter began her relationship with the Town Plan and Zoning Commission (TPZ) through her appointment as secretary to the TPZ in the 1960s. She worked with the TPZ and other town boards for several years before working in her current capacity. Her knowledge of the permit process ranges from a thorough understanding of legal issues to a well-developed intuition for the concerns that will be raised by board members.

Involving the private sector   Bloomfield's Economic Development Commission (EDC) serves as an advisory committee on economic development policy and programs. Its five members, appointed by the town manager, currently include the president of a local bank, one large corporation executive, one small businessman, a builder and manager of shopping centers, and a developer of industrial property. This group mainly promotes and sells parcels of land in the municipally owned Blue Hills Industrial Park. However, the EDC not only promotes the Blue Hills properties, but also seeks tenants for other vacant industrial land.

The EDC also helps develop promotional materials, working with a former media person who was hired by the town to assist in promotion. One of the most successful activities of the EDC is an on-going series of luncheons and dinners which serve as a catalyst for civic pride among current owners, as well as an introduction to Bloomfield for potential businesses, developers, and area realtors. While data about Bloomfield's vacant parcels and community advantages is provided to participants, the most important aspect of these activities is the chance for Bloomfield's government and current and prospective businesses to talk together. Some of the functions that have been held include:

1. A luncheon for Connecticut industrial and commerical realtors featuring a film of Bloomfield and comments by town officials
2. A dinner honoring the 100 top taxpayers of Bloomfield (which are all business concerns)
3. A luncheon for the municipally owned industrial park land owners, renters, and prospective tenants.

Program management: the role of the town manager   The basic issue that Bloomfield faced in responding to its business community's needs is a familiar one. The problems of business and industry cut across the departmental jurisdictions traditionally used in the provision of services like police and fire protection, zoning and building code enforcement, and environmental regulation. For the new program to be effective, the individuals who staffed the positions needed to be able to command authority; without that authority, the town's ombudsman and expediter would have little credibility with individuals in the private sector. Bloomfield's solution was to make its industrial development program a staff function within the town manager's office.

The town manager credited this decision as one of the most important steps on the program's road to success. Interdepartmental disputes over the priority for requests put through by program staffers are rare. "The departments know that the request comes from the boss's office; that the staff is working directly for me." Bloomfield has a tradition of strong town managers, which makes this type of control functional. Another reason for the program's success is that the manager makes it clear that business development is *his* priority by devoting an estimated 20–25 percent of his time to economic development activities. His work includes the following tasks:

1. He joins in a bi-weekly staff review of current development proposals.
2. He provides direction to staff.
3. He provides information on new policy options and program development to elected officials.

4. He meets personally with developers, owners, state officials, and others when his staff feels it would be helpful.

The manager's personal commitment has an impact on town employees and helps define priorities. But he feels there is an added advantage in having the program located in his office—industries interested in Bloomfield are favorably impressed by dealing with the chief appointed official in the community.

Bloomfield's long-standing interest in economic development can be traced to the community's desire, expressed through its elected officials' policies, to hold down the tax burden on home-owners.

Program oversight: the role of elected officials   Bloomfield's elected officials are kept informed of economic development program activities through reports from the town manager. Their direct interest in the program is evidenced by their participation in the luncheon and dinner meetings which EDC sponsors. At these meetings, council representatives distribute themselves among the dining tables to chat with the present and potential owners of industry and commerce in their community.

Identifying and utilizing local resources

Bloomfield's program is straightforward in design and in practice. Its primary goal is the growth of tax ratables. Bloomfield does not seek to diversify its economic base in terms of specific kinds of industry, although current efforts are focused on attracting firms which will provide job opportunities for blue-collar workers. There is a sense, unconfirmed by data analysis, that any growth (with the exception of heavily polluting industry) is good for the community. Because Bloomfield continues to experience growth, its program of expediting permits, improving the provision of services, and marketing its significant amounts of vacant land (most serviced by utilities) is working well.

The quality of life   Bloomfield's staff is clearly aware of the importance that quality of life issues play in attracting industry. The staff speaks enthusiastically of Bloomfield's integrated neighborhoods, its wide range of housing types and prices, its schools, open space, and pleasant retail center. Local commitment to enhancing the quality of life is clear in this example: recognizing the local school system's high-quality music program, Bloomfield officials worked with executives of Connecticut General Life Insurance Company to offer summer symphonies by major artists on the rolling lawns of the company's headquarters. The town manager stated, "We want Bloomfield's name to trigger this kind of association in people's minds."

Available land   Because Bloomfield has many acres of vacant land to market, its activities in this area are strong. Data on available parcels is comprehensive and up-to-date, and the land is actively marketed by the Economic Development Commission. In an attempt to make the municipally owned industrial parcels more competitive, the EDC decided to drop the selling price from $20,000 per acre to $10,000. While parcels in other areas of the community average close to $20,000 per acre, this step was taken because the EDC requires quality building design and landscaping, which is more expensive for developers.

Dollars for development   Bloomfield operates from an advantageous position, since the private sector continues to view the market as strong and is willing to invest. One bank president commented that "capital has never been a problem in Bloomfield." This comment is confirmed by the town manager, who states that tax abatements or other forms of financial assistance are not needed as incentives to encourage companies to locate in Bloomfield. Town staff have made contacts with state officials, however, and introduce individuals who request assistance to individuals in the Connecticut Economic Development Authority.

Building the labor force   Because of the community's location within the Hartford metropolitan area, it draws on a large labor force rich in all types of crafts and skills. The town also works to develop the local labor force. Bloomfield's high school offers a cooperative work experience program, placing students in local businesses to help them explore alternatives, choose realistic goals, and learn how to achieve these goals. The town sees this as a "unique program and another example of how Bloomfield industry and government help each other." To show its own commitment to this program, the town also provides a number of student placements in the town hall.

In summary, Bloomfield strengthens its position relative to other communities by:

1. Reducing risk in the development permit processes
2. Providing information on local development opportunities
3. Providing contacts at state agencies when needed
4. Ensuring that public services are provided as efficiently as possible.

These activities, funded through the town budget, show businesses that Bloomfield is interested in growth.

Program evaluation

Bloomfield has not attempted to identify how much of the community's business growth is related to its program. The community's officials are proud that the program meets the goals of equalizing the residential/business sector tax burden and creates a strong public/private relationship.

The tangible results   Since the inception of the 1974 program, growth has occurred in the following areas:

1. Industries, including office space, have expanded or are now expanding to a total of 940,622 square feet.
2. Commercial enterprises have expanded or are now expanding to a total of 80,181 square feet.
3. Tax base ratables in industrial and commercial properties have risen from $75 million to $89 million.
4. There has been an increase in employment in Bloomfield from 13,700 to 15,180 (in the Hartford region, the increase has been from 347,840 to 375,520).

The intangibles   Bloomfield has found that the time and effort involved in operating this program generate tangible benefits (jobs and ratables) and intangible benefits (the goodwill of industries and professionals who have worked with the town). The two-way communication between the business community and town has stopped the "surprise exits" of industries which frustrate many communities. Moreover, as the town manager said, "our best ambassadors are the businessmen themselves." When interested industries call to learn about the community, the staff frequently refers them to individuals in large and small companies for direct information on how businesses are treated in Bloomfield. The result? After such referrals, companies have called back to say "I called three of the names you gave me . . . I'm sold!"

A similar but less direct goodwill result is expressed by architects and engineers who praise the effectiveness of Bloomfield's development permit process. The president of a firm of landscape architects sent a letter saying, "In short, the entire procedure is very conducive to creative and sensible design and encourages applicants and designers to do their best." These feelings have resulted in engineers and architects suggesting Bloomfield as a location to other clients.

The EDC-sponsored luncheons and dinners have resulted in a number of warm, appreciative letters from local business showing the positive impact that such a program can have. One example is a letter from a realtor who wrote: "Your presentation of Bloomfield stimulated my enthusiasm for your community. Now when I speak of Bloomfield, I can better emphasize the qualities that provoke such elephantine enthusiasm from your community."

Annual program costs   Bloomfield funds its business development activities directly through the local budget. The costs of the

Program costs, 1979	
Staff salaries	$20,240
20% of manager's salary	
20% of assistant manager's salary	
15% of administrative assistant's salary	
15% of community relations staff salary	
Transportation	260
Economic Development Committee	20,000
Luncheons and dinners	
Promotional materials and mailing	———
Total costs, 1979	$40,500

program (see box) represent direct outlays based on the Economic Development Committee's budget, transportation costs of the ombudsman program, and percentages of staff salaries relative to the amount of time spent on business development. Other costs, such as building space costs, are considered to be minimal by the town staff and are not calculated.

The bottom line   It is hard to measure effectively the dollar costs and benefits of a program which has a major goal of improving business attitudes toward local government. It appears successful, it meets the goals that elected officials have set, and has resulted in a less cumbersome permit process which has made developers happier and lightened the load of the town boards by making the process flow more smoothly. Is it worth the cost—both the dollars and the time outlay that cannot be spent on other community needs? The town manager's response to this question leaves no doubt about his feelings, and is representative of the attitude that a visitor perceives throughout the town's staff. "The time spent on industrial development," he says, "is the *best* investment Bloomfield has made."

Negotiating Business Development: The Manager As Broker

Cheryl A. Farr and Lawrence D. Rose

The following case study describes how the city of Mercer Island, Washington, negotiated a particularly novel land development deal, and how the city manager functioned as an effective broker in the negotiations.

Background

The city of Mercer Island is a lovely island in the middle of Lake Washington, linked to Seattle on the west and its sprawling suburbs to the east by the bridges of interstate highway I-90. In 1978, the city's population of 22,000 was predominantly well-to-do; recent sales of island homes had a mean value of $146,000. Mercer Island's winding roads, lovely vistas, and breathtakingly attractive residences had earned it a reputation as a wealthy community.

The city government, however, was far from being comparably wealthy. This can be traced in some measure to the fact that the business district was quite small and contained mostly service enterprises such as service stations, grocery stores, dry cleaners, and drug stores; sales and business taxes produced limited revenue. But in even larger measure, the economic straits of the city can be traced to a state law, passed in 1973, which effectively deprived the city of much of the value of the rich and expanding assessment roll that had been the basis for property (ad valorem) taxes, the former keystone of Mercer Island's revenue system. That law limited all cities in the state to collecting no more than 106 percent of the prop-

This is an updated version of *Negotiating Business Development: The Manager As a Broker in Land Development*, Municipal Innovations Series, no. 34 (Washington, D.C.: International City Management Association, 1981). The report was supported by a grant from the Economic Development Administration (#99-06-07024-1).

erty tax dollars received in the preceding year. Accordingly, tax rates became merely an expression of dollars, not a measure of revenue to be produced.

Mercer Island has faced the problems of inflation and rising costs with a property tax revenue base that expands slowly and, correspondingly, with an increasing interest in the revenues to be gained from utility taxes, business and operating taxes, and the 0.5 percent sales tax the city receives from local sales. In evaluating the avenues that would provide needed revenues, local officials saw few real choices. Because of the property tax cap, residential development was not an encouraging option. Development had spread south in waves across the island for two decades, leaving few available residential sites. Since the city had developed over the years the image of a place that valued attractive amenities and quality of life attributes, officials did not consider industrial uses as an option for revenue development. City officials became convinced that attractively designed commercial and office development was the only means to increase local sales tax revenue and thereby provide needed services for residents. They believed that Mercer Island's location (ten minutes from downtown Seattle), as well as its affluent market, would encourage such development.

In the early seventies, the city drafted its first master plan. Among the stated goals was the development of a healthy economy in the main business district, an eleven-block area containing a fragmented collection of buildings heavily punctuated with parking lots. Most of the buildings were occupied by wholesale, retail, and professional office uses. While the vacancy rate was low, much of the commerce was marginally successful and the turnover rate was high.

The major undertaking proposed in the master plan to generate a healthier economy in this central business district was the construction of a city hall and community center. A fourteen-acre parcel of land belonging to the school district, which was vacant and not expected to be needed in the future, was pinpointed as the appropriate place. For years it had been zoned exclusively for public purposes. The schools had no need for the site, but the city had no means to acquire it or to develop something on it even if the site were acquired.

At one point, it seemed that what was called for in the master plan—a new city hall and community center, and downtown revitalization generally—could be accomplished. The city had submitted a grant proposal to the Economic Development Administration (EDA) and the school district's board had agreed to lease the property to the city for a token amount if the EDA grant came through. It did not, however, and the idea of a new city hall went on the back burner. Occasionally city officials speculated about doing something with four acres owned by the city immediately adjoining the school property. But "doing something" required money, and the city treasury was conspicuously missing the resources needed to do anything. A portion of the city-owned four acres was being used by the city's water and sewer utility, but this was seen as an inefficient use of valuable property and was considered a temporary situation until the resources needed to develop the site materialized.

Repeated efforts during the seventies demonstrate the city's continuous commitment to the economic development goal the master plan had set. The city implemented commercial development design controls which enhanced the aesthetic appeal of the central business district by setting design standards for the service and convenience businesses that were built. The city also committed the business and occupation tax revenues it collected to a business district beautification fund. Through the fund utilities were placed underground, attractive street lighting was purchased, and plantings and street furniture were placed in easements along property edges. For council members, new and old, city manager Larry Rose consistently highlighted the master plan's goal of economic growth and kept alive an awareness of the central business district's sales tax potential. The political commitment to economic development downtown remained strong, with officials awaiting the right opportunity.

Summer of 1979: the turning point   In the summer of 1979, Mercer Island's officials faced twin problems. The first, and most difficult, was that the city's corporation yard, housing the public works facilities, was located on leased space in the path of highway construction and had to be vacated. As the officials looked for new space, they realized quickly that Mercer Island's little remaining vacant land was too expensive to purchase; furthermore, no available sites would adequately screen this unattractive use from nearby residential areas. The only available city-owned land was the four-acre parcel in the central business district. City officials believed that the corporation yard would be an unwise use of valuable property, and even began looking for a site in an adjacent community.

It was at this point that a phone call to the mayor presented a second, less difficult problem. In retrospect, however, this call precipitated events that are seen as a turning point for the expansion of Mercer Island's economic base.

That historic call came from Charles Bershears, then president of one of Mercer Island's major employers, Farmers New World Life Insurance Company. He was seeking help from Mayor Ben Werner in solving a problem his company had (and one the city would have liked to have had): how to manage business growth. The problem that Bershears presented to the mayor had to do with expanding the company's parking facilities into the residential zone. The under-standable opinion Farmers had received from city staff was that it was unlikely that the zoning law would be amended for this purpose. Bershears asked the mayor if anything could be done. The mayor, in turn, suggested that city manager Rose talk with Bershears to see what help, if any, could be offered.

From the city's perspective, as Rose initially saw it, the depar-ture of the company would have very little impact. Insurance com-panies and banks in the state of Washington are regulated and taxed totally by the state, so the city received no direct revenues from this business. Although there were almost 800 people working in the Farmers office building, its freeway location meant that the vast majority of employees went to and from work on the freeway, and seldom used the services in the business district. As this was a conclusion that nobody disputed, there simply seemed to be no jus-tification for a time-consuming effort, even for a firm which for years had been a respectable corporate citizen.

Then, it dawned on Rose one day. If Farmers could stay on the island but be relocated to the central business district, its payroll of 800 employees and the purchasing power they represented could provide a dynamic boost for the entire economy of the city. The fourteen-acre property belonging to the school district suddenly, once again, loomed as critically important.

The plight of Farmers, a subsidiary of the Los Angeles–based Farmers Insurance Group, was real and becoming more onerous day by day. The spectacular growth of the business compelled it to expand almost immediately. The company had sufficient land at the present site, which had been bought in the mid-1950s, but zoning bisected it. The front 4.8 acres, on which the Farmers building was situated, were zoned commercial/office; the southerly 9 acres were zoned residential. The company had failed to seek a change in the zoning classification at the time of purchase, when it probably would have been simple to do so. This was not the case in 1979.

Farmers had engaged the services of a respected local land at-torney to explore the possibility of the rezoning early in 1979. After talking with city officials and residents in the neighborhood sur-rounding the site, the attorney advised Farmers that there was sub-stantial opposition, that the process might consume the better part of a year, and that the outcome was uncertain. Farmers could not wait a year, especially for an unpredictable result. Already bulging at the seams, the company had to begin at once to provide for expan-sion, and the only certain alternative was to go elsewhere—out to the suburbs, where land would be inexpensive and plentiful. In fact the board of directors had already decided to relocate to the suburbs at the time the city had come on the scene. This was not a promising situation for the city to try to change the course of destiny.

Negotiating a public-private partnership

Assuming that the fourteen-acre school property would still be available at the generous terms agreed to when the city had applied for the EDA grant, Rose discussed with Mayor Werner the idea of making available to Farmers the school site plus the adjoining four acres owned by the city. On this land Farmers could build its headquarters and a city hall which the city could lease back. Or the city could build the complex, using revenue bonds, and lease space to Farmers.

Mayor Werner urged Rose to make the proposal to Bershears, which he did. Bershears, who wanted to remain on the island for sentimental as well as practical reasons, discussed it with his directors. Later he told Rose there was some interest among board members, and asked Rose if he would be willing to go to Los Angeles and lay the plan before the full board of the parent company. Informal discussion and casual suggestion had suddenly taken on a serious note.

Rose needed not only authority to proceed; he needed a competent endorsement of the validity of the plan. At a meeting arranged by Mayor Werner, key members of the city council were joined by James Ellis, a distinguished Seattle bond attorney. Ellis, a champion of public-private cooperation who had put together some nationally renowned projects, gave enthusiastic support to the proposal. And the council members approved the idea of having Rose make the offer to Farmers' board of directors.

At the board of directors' meeting, several issues were critical in bringing about the positive response Rose received:

1. The city manager was able to be frank about why Mercer Island was offering its proposal: 800 warm bodies with discretionary income to spend would be working daily in the downtown area.

2. The city had "done its homework," having gone to a reputable lawyer for legal advice *before* it went to the Farmers Insurance Group's board of directors. A key board member who knew Ellis told his colleagues, "If Jim Ellis says it's a good deal, I believe it is."

3. The insurance company knew that if it left Mercer Island it would lose roughly 25 percent of its existing employees. Insurance companies are labor intensive, with a heavy dependence on relatively low-paying clerical jobs. Employees were unhappy at the thought of a longer drive, which would increase both commuting time and expenses. Mercer Island provided a broader labor market to draw from than a distant suburb, and the downtown site had the added advantage of being on an intercity bus route. The company preferred to find a site close enough to its present location to enable it to

keep most of the employees, rather than face extensive training of new employees.

4. The city manager emphasized that Mercer Island wanted to keep Farmers and would work cooperatively with the company, while many of the distant suburbs were antagonistic toward business development. He mentioned that Farmers could face environmental restrictions and citizen scrutiny in a developing community, whereas because Mercer Island's site was in a developed commercial area where the master plan called for additional growth, the likelihood of such problems was much lower.

The Farmers Insurance Group's board of directors was interested, and agreed that Mercer Island's officials should negotiate with the school district for its fourteen-acre parcel. However, Farmers would continue evaluating alternative sites for its new facility in case the Mercer Island site did not come available.

Mercer Island is unusual in that the school district and city borders are coterminous, but it is not unusual in having a weak relationship with the school board. Because much of the school board's budget is provided through the state of Washington, it was relatively unconcerned about the local government's revenue needs or economic development goals.

After three months of negotiations with the school board, Mercer Island's officials concluded that the proposal they had made to Farmers was not going to work. The school board did not want to part with its land without receiving a substantial payment—perhaps as much as $3 million. Because the school board had never obligated itself to sell its fourteen acres to the city at the time of the EDA proposal for a new city hall, the city did not have any choice but to pay the asking price or give up hope of getting the site. (The school district's land was zoned for public use and could not be sold for commercial use by the school board.)

City officials were frustrated at not being able to bring the school district's site into the deal, but were unwilling to give up hope. They searched for another way to bring the Farmers payroll into Mercer Island's central business district. Taking a fresh look at the situation, local officials came up with another idea. On the side of the city's four-acre parcel opposite the school district's property was a two-acre site occupied by a bowling alley. The city manager remembered hearing that the owner wanted to sell. Could a building meeting Farmers' need be accommodated on six acres?

The city decided to try to make it work. Mercer Island's city council made a bold move: it voted $20,000 to hire an architectural firm called TRA to do a massing study to determine if a building suiting Farmers' needs could be accommodated on a six-acre site. Farmers had hired TRA to do preliminary drawings of buildings suiting its need, although no site had been chosen. The prospective building would have to meet the requirements of the local design review board, provide on-site parking, and not block the views of Lake Washington that were a selling point for unit owners in the adjacent condominium complex. At the same time, the council voted to take a one-year option to buy the bowling alley site. The $5,000 earnest money deposit would be forfeited if the site was not purchased.

City manager Rose told Farmers president Bershears what the city intended to do, but did not try to elicit any promises from the company in exchange. The city council believed that bringing a major employment center into the central business district was important enough to the community to merit risking some of the city's limited funds. Farmers was impressed with this public-sector commitment.

Developing public support   While the TRA massing study was being developed, the manager and mayor put together a "crisis team" composed of representatives of the design review board, the planning commission, and the city council. The crisis team was briefed on the city's proposal to Farmers and the plans in the works. When TRA completed its efforts the crisis team, under the guidance of Jerry Bacon, director of community development, met with the manager and the mayor to discuss the six design alternatives that TRA had proposed. Working from the six sketches, the crisis team and TRA created a building design that met the criteria of Farmers, the design review board, the planning commission, and the city council.

Hoping that when TRA had completed its massing drawing one or more of the concepts would prove attractive to Farmers, local officials continued to ruminate about an alternative deal to be negotiated. A new city hall could wait, but a new corporation yard could not. Finally, the city settled on the idea of trading the city's six acres for Farmers' fourteen acres. While it could be postulated that land values were about equal because the city's six acres had more valuable zoning, the Farmers office building was obviously an asset of enormous value. So what the city finally focused on was not the value of the building as part of a trade, but its value if Farmers had to sell that building and property and pay capital gains taxes on it. Why not give the building to the city and create a tax write-off?

City officials again sought out the best resource person available to help evaluate that possibility. The city manager called on Hugo Oswald, a corporate tax attorney and a former member of the city's planning commission. Explaining the negotiations that had taken place, Rose asked Oswald to review the tax consequences for Farmers of a land swap combined with a donation of its building to the city for use as a city hall. While Oswald obviously did not have information on Farmers' particular tax situation, he was able to provide a generic analysis of the proposal's tax consequences.

Oswald's analysis highlighted several options providing favorable tax consequences for the business. For all the options, the crux of the analysis was this: because Farmers had owned the property since the early fifties and property values had risen dramatically in the intervening years, Farmers would face a large capital gains tax upon the sale of its property. By giving its building to the city, Farmers would be able to take a charitable deduction off its tax liability. The deductions could be taken over five years, so the high value of the property could be written off against corporate tax liabilities in increments. By swapping Farmers' land for publicly owned land of equal value, no gain or loss would be recognized from the land swap by the Internal Revenue Service.

With the documentation from the massing study and the corporate tax analysis backing up its proposal, the city was ready to offer Farmers an attractive package. The city would exercise its option to buy the bowling alley property by issuing a $3 million councilmanic general obligation bond for a new city hall and corporation yard. Seven hundred thousand dollars would be used for purchasing the bowling alley site, $1.5 million would finance construction of a new corporation yard, and $400,000 would be held in reserve by the city. The city would clear the two adjoining central business district sites and trade them for Farmers' two adjoining sites (i.e., the commercially zoned and the residentially zoned parcels). The parcels would be assumed equal in value, so no gain or loss would be recognized from the land swap. Farmers would donate its building to the city as a charitable gift, and the city (as it thought at the time) would renovate it for use as a city hall. The city's corporation yard would be built on the nine-acre parcel behind the old Farmers building. Farmers would build its new building on the central business district site.

As the deal moved from idea toward reality, city officials worked to anticipate and avoid problems. Early on, the city manager met with the local newspaper editor to brief her on the city's negotiations. Appreciating the fact that private corporations shy away from publicity about inconclusive negotiations and might be scared off by premature public speculation—and thus be lost to the city as an economic boon—the editor agreed to hold back the story until negotiations were firm. However, she did write a stirring editorial that stated that Farmers was thinking about moving because of its expansion needs and that urged city officials and residents to work together to keep a fine corporate citizen on the island. This timely editorial was effective in nurturing public support for the city's efforts and in increasing Farmers' understanding of its local support.

After the city received preliminary drawings from TRA and

met with the crisis team to pick a good design, the community development director and the city manager began meeting with the condominium associations from buildings near the site to explain the proposal and its impact on the condominium sites. Thanks to the geographical configuration of the island (the central business district sits low near the shore and is surrounded on the other three sides by terraced slopes), the proposed five-story Farmers building would not obscure the condominiums' lake view. In addition, the new development would replace the city's utility company facility and an old bowling alley with an attractively designed employment center. This public relations effort paid off; the condominium associations were, on balance, not opposed to the project.

As the negotiations evolved into a legal agreement for the exchange of property, the deal wavered on the edge of an abyss. Lawyers for both parties worked to hammer out an agreement, but their inclinations to protect their clients threatened to smother the deal in layer upon layer of clauses and exceptions. City manager Rose called Harold Gingrich, the corporate vice president for real estate investments, who had taken charge of Farmers' end of the negotiations. Backed by the knowledge that the city council had given him the power to negotiate the deal to its conclusion, Rose was able to come quickly to the point.

"Harold," Rose said, "the lawyers are asking for all kinds of things we never discussed. Can you tell me exactly what you want?"

Gingrich replied, "We'll swap the lands and give you the building."

"You've got a deal!" said Rose.

There was a long pause. "I have?" asked Gingrich.

"Yes," said Rose. "Now would you please call your lawyers and tell them that's the deal and nothing else?"

Gingrich did just that.

The legal agreement   The agreement that developed between the city and Farmers focused on three major issues: the property exchange, the charitable gift, and the building permit and closing date.

Property exchange   The city of Mercer Island and Farmers agreed that their lands were equivalent in value, and so qualified as a tax-free exchange under the provisions of Section 1031 of the Internal Revenue Code of 1954, as amended. This was important to Farmers because it allowed the company to avoid a capital gains tax. It was advantageous to both the city and Farmers because it resulted in a direct exchange with no cash involved, and both parties were getting property more valuable to them than the property they were giving up.

If the downtown parcel proved to be unsuitable for Farmers'

proposed development as a result of soils and engineering tests, the city would receive Farmers' nine-acre, residentially zoned site in exchange for the two-acre bowling alley site. The city would be able to build its corporation yard, and Farmers would be able to sell or lease the cleared bowling alley property at its discretion. The location of the bowling alley site made it a valuable piece of real estate for investment purposes; on the other hand the nine acres Farmers owned were unusable for corporate purposes, and too close to offices and the highway to yield a quick sale for residential use.

Charitable gift   Farmers, "because of its long and beneficial association with the Mercer Island community," and because it "was aware of the desperate need of the city for adequate municipal facilities," gave its existing building to the city as a charitable gift. This gift, the agreement noted, "was neither a part of nor consideration for the property exchange." In this way, the city received a building to use for municipal facilities and Farmers was able to offset other corporate tax liabilities with the value of its gift. It should be noted that a gifting like this will only appeal to companies with enough tax liability to make the gifting worthwhile, *and* with enough funds available to cover new construction without selling its existing building. For Farmers, this was the case.

Building permit and closing date   Because no guarantee was given by the city that Farmers would get the permits necessary to build, the agreement was made contingent upon Farmers receiving a permit and turning its building over to the city by a specified date. If, for any reason, Farmers did not receive a permit, the deal would revert to the exchange of the residentially zoned site for the bowling alley site. The city required a specific closing date to ensure that Farmers carried out its end of the bargain in a timely fashion.

The agreement was signed, and soon construction began on Farmers' new building, and on the city's new corporation yard. A $15,000 sculpture jointly commissioned by the city of Mercer Island and Farmers New World Life Insurance Company was erected in the plaza in front of the new Farmers headquarters as a monument to the public-private partnership that had made the new development possible.

Afterword   As the city evaluated its space needs, it concluded that the old Farmers building was not suitable for a city hall because its floor space of 37,000 square feet was 20,000 square feet more than the city would be able to use. There was also concern that the former corporate headquarters was a bit too ostentatious for a city hall.

The city officials decided to seek a tenant to lease the building. An independent real estate company estimated the lease could bring in as much as $270,000–$300,000 per year. The city would be required to pay a 12 percent leasehold tax on any lease revenues since the building would be leased for private purposes, but the right tenant might also provide a high sales tax revenue for the city. Sales tax in the state is levied at the point of sale, so a corporate office can provide significant sales tax revenues; and the local share of 0.5 percent of sales taxes collected could add significantly to local revenues. The council decided to make a serious effort to market the building, and dedicated a major portion of the city manager's time to it. It was expected that revenue from the lease would service the debt on construction of a new city hall when a suitable site became available.

Mercer Island's ownership of the old Farmers building theoretically gave the city the capability to choose a desirable tenant, but the effects of the recession in 1981 and 1982 made it impossible to find any tenant able to afford the space at the estimated rate. Unwilling to leave the building empty until the economy improved, the city council leased the space to the state department of transportation for five years at a below-market rate (which would nonetheless produce over $1 million). The council planned to rent the building more profitably later to a commercial tenant.

In the meantime, however, a surprising new land swap has been negotiated. The city council agreed to exchange the old Farmers building for the school district parcel located in the central business district—the fourteen-acre parcel that the city first identified in the early seventies as the appropriate site for a city hall and community center. The school district urgently needed income, and the council voted to make the exchange "for the good of the schools."

Now the city is faced once again with the problem of what to do with an undeveloped, but valuable, property in the central business district, without money to do much of anything. The school parcel is still zoned for park and public uses only. It is the largest undeveloped parcel in the central business district, and the council is aware that its development will have a profound influence on the economic, social, and cultural health of the city.

Once Farmers moved into its new building, downtown land values began to rise, from $6-$7 per square foot in 1979 to $8-$12 per square foot in 1981, to $18-$20 per square foot in 1984. Pressures have mounted to rezone contiguous single-family parcels to multifamily. Although 1,000 people are now employed by Farmers at the new location, the effect on shops and stores nearby has been difficult to assess.

The city council would like to use the large downtown property it now owns to give the still random business community a strong, colorful, and distinctive character, supportive of and supported by a magnetic civic, cultural, and social presence. A joint public-private venture that would give the city the financial wherewithal it needs to develop the property seems the most likely option available. Whether the citizens of Mercer Island will tolerate any commercial use of the site (probably an inevitable result of public-private development) is an unanswered question at present. With land values up (partly because of the new Farmers headquarters) the city does not judge it economical to sell the property and go into the market for another site for a city hall complex. Another question complicating the city's planning is whether the central business district can tolerate competition from new commercial office space. If the city should build commercial office space on its new property, would it ruin the market for private interests? To find some answers to these questions and plan the best use for the new parcel, the council has appointed a committee that includes representatives of the city's business interests. The council is determined to pursue the public-private approach, which proved so successful four years ago in relocating the city's corporation yard and keeping a valuable business in the city.

Evaluation team's assessment

Shortly after the exchange of the old Farmers building for the city's six-acre site in the spring of 1981, an evaluation team sponsored by ICMA visited Mercer Island to evaluate the transferability, to other small and medium-sized cities, of elements that were critical to this public-private land development process. The team looked at the project from two perspectives: the deal itself and the role of the manager as a broker in land development negotiations.

The deal itself In considering the transferability of elements in the deal itself, the team believed that this project exemplified the use of three techniques:

Land swap Two publicly owned sites and two privately owned sites considered equal in value were traded. The exchange of such sites qualifies as a like-kind exchange under Section 1031 of the Internal Revenue Code of 1954, as amended. (This section provides that no gain or loss is recognized when properties of like kind are exchanged.) Since Section 1031 does not state that both parties must be taxpayers normally subject to taxation, involvement of a municipal tax-exempt corporation as one of the parties to the agreement does not affect the usefulness of Section 1031. The review team noted that there was no requirement for a professional appraisal of the land value to determine similar value.

Mercer Island's land swap took place so that the city and the insurance company could construct buildings on sites that were more appropriate for their new development than the sites the parties originally owned. But this is not the only situation in which swaps can be effective. For example, land swaps also can be used by communities to *prevent* the development of a specific site. This can be done by exchanging a publicly owned parcel that is considered appropriate for private development, for a privately owned site, and then restricting the use of the newly acquired site to public open space.

A technique similar to land swaps is transferring air rights to offer investors developable space while maintaining public control of the site. In some cases local governments have then used the land at or below ground level to provide a development incentive (e.g., building a public parking garage underground). This will reduce development costs for the developer by providing on-site parking, and will provide revenue to the community. Lease payments and property taxes on the air space and improvements can provide communities with additional revenues, and at the same time the communities can retain control of the land.

Charitable gift   The review team noted that the large, successful private corporation involved in the Mercer Island deal had been unaware of the favorable tax consequences that would result from donating its building to a municipality. The team noted that such deductions on taxable income can be very attractive to corporations that have tax liabilities to offset yet do not need cash from the sale of their buildings for other purposes.

City officials frequently assume that private corporations are familiar with every trick in the book as far as development goes, but that is not always the case. The review team emphasized that local officials should realize that since businesses move infrequently they may welcome ideas for different approaches that can be used for development. The team noted that companies make mistakes just as cities do, but because they do not operate in the public eye their errors are not as well publicized as the public sector's.

School district–local government cooperation   Although the negotiations between the city of Mercer Island and its school district broke down, the concept of communities acquiring excess school property is transferable. Many school districts had projected higher population growth rates than have materialized and are left with both buildings and undeveloped sites that exceed their future needs. School districts may be willing to sell or lease these properties to the local government at minimal cost.

The manager as broker   In evaluating the manager's role as a broker in public-private land development negotiations, the review team highlighted several points as being important for other communities and managers undertaking similar activities.

A positive manager-council relationship   First and foremost in importance for successful negotiations is the need for a strong, supportive mayor-manager relationship. The manager in Mercer Island had the trust of the council, and particularly of the mayor. Decisions were made through continuous consultation between the manager and the mayor. The council members trusted the mayor to keep an eye on the day-to-day proceedings, and at every critical point the full council discussed its members' concerns and made the decisions. Without the knowledge that the council had given him its approval to negotiate a deal, the city manager could not have functioned effectively.

A willingness to get the facts that make good ideas persuasive arguments Cities should not expect the private sector to do its own homework. If a project or a deal is important enough, the public sector should be willing to risk some of its own funds to explore options and to buttress its ideas with facts. Team members agreed that it is worth the expense to buy the best expertise the community can afford. Talented, imaginative resource people provide credibility that reduces the perceived risk in novel undertakings. Each time Mercer Island's local officials came up with what they thought might be a good approach they sought professionals, who were known in their field, to back up the city's ideas with facts, and this paid off. The city also put its own money at risk—in the option to buy the bowling alley site, and in commissioning TRA's massing study.

Being honest and following through on promises Private sector representatives often are wary of involvement with the public sector, either because they have been "burned" once before or have heard of another business that was mistreated in a public-private partnership. Continued demonstration of good intent and not promising what cannot be delivered are the cornerstones for building public-private partnerships. The city manager's efforts to conclude negotiations quickly and efficiently through careful preparation and follow-through avoided the costly bureaucratic delays that the private sector often associates with government "help."

Implementing established policy A consensus on the need for economic growth should be developed well in advance of any specific deal. If managers wait until the opportunity presents itself, it can be too late to mobilize support. When deciding which deals are worth investing the time and trouble to negotiate, the first question should be: "Is it in the master or comprehensive plan?" If not, said the review team, either it should be put in the plan or it isn't worth a major effort. When the type of development under negotiation is in an approved master plan, that document backs up the manager's stand. Then he or she is simply implementing established policy. City manager Rose recognized the need for consensus building, and directed his efforts toward orienting new council members to the master plan's economic development goals, and also reminding longtime council members of these goals.

Negotiating requires a team effort   Council support in negotiating public-private partnerships is one key ingredient; a second is staff support, needed to overcome minor obstacles that can torpedo an otherwise perfect proposal. Unless the task has been designated to a specific staff person, the manager should provide leadership in brokering public-private partnerships and set the tone for the staff's approach. At some point in most public-private land development negotiations someone from the public sector needs to tell naysayers, "We want this to work. Don't tell me why it can't work, show me how it *can*." For important deals it is also useful to develop a team that can expedite the project through the procedural slowdowns that inevitably occur.

Retaining existing businesses makes sense   Keeping industries that are already located in a community is easier than bringing in new ones. More time should be spent by communities in helping existing industries stay or expand than in chasing down new leads. Recent studies show that very few businesses actually relocate each year, and the likelihood of a positive outcome is much higher when the business has a vested interest in the community.

Learning the art of negotiating   Regardless of the amount of legwork the manager does, the council is taking the public risk, and council members deserve the lion's share of credit for deals the manager successfully brokers. It is also important to keep in mind that some deals just will not work, and creating a crisis can harm a manager's future in a community. Managers can function effectively as brokers of public authority and property only in a harmonious environment; they must develop an intuition not only for when to call it quits in fruitless negotiations, but for when to get out of the limelight.

Anticipating roadblocks   There are many powers to contend with in public-private partnerships: the client, the staff, the city council, the media, the legal counsel, the citizens affected by the deal, the common good, and the manager's personal desire to mold the deal. Managers need to be imaginative, both in identifying their communities' negotiating strengths and in anticipating potential stumbling blocks. There were several points in Mercer Island's negotiations where the city's officials might easily have thrown in the towel. Perseverance, imagination, and hard work helped them win their fight.

Negotiating land development deals takes time   On Mercer Island the private corporation was unable to handle its business without additional space, and the city faced eviction from its leased corporation yard. The deal came together quite easily because both sides needed to close the negotiations quickly. Even so, it still took nearly a year to get a signed agreement. The manager must have the council's backing to spend an inordinate amount of time negotiating the details of a project, or must have a staff person available to do the legwork.

Conclusion
Communities interested in encouraging local economic growth through public-private land development partnerships must make a long-range commitment of staff time, political support, and local funds to reap the rewards they seek. Mercer Island's project shows that cities can negotiate successfully for desired business development without using tax abatements or industrial revenue bonds, and without relying on federal or state funding.

Local government administrators who have worked as public-private land development brokers emphasize that the key to their effectiveness is council support. This frees them from much of the crisis management of day-to-day administration of their communities, and allows them to commit the community to a deal. They also note that negotiating land development deals is enjoyable and challenging; the bricks-and-mortar results give a different sense of accomplishment than most other tasks local administrators undertake.

The need for imaginative approaches for revenue development is likely to increase the opportunity for local government administrators to be the front runners in entrepreneurial cities. It is the responsibility of managers to communicate the need for a team approach to their councils, and to develop and maintain with them the positive relationships that are critical in successful public-private land development negotiations.

Keeping Investment Dollars Home

Business leaders in Chippewa Falls, Wisconsin, have come up with an extremely successful method of attracting new industry. In 1976, they purchased an Illinois firm with private funds and moved its manufacturing plant to their city. A recent plant addition, funded cooperatively through local government and private investors, has brought the total number of jobs created by this initiative to over 80.

The story in Chippewa Falls illustrates how small communities can benefit when citizens pool their funds for economic development and investment dollars are kept at home.

Chippewa Falls is a growing city of 12,000 in northwest Wisconsin. Local leaders attribute the community's steady prosperity to the cooperation among city officials, lending institutions and the business community. For nearly 30 years, the city's industrial development corporation has been instrumental in local development efforts and in marketing the city's commercial advantage throughout Wisconsin and neighboring states. The Mason Shoe Company and the Seymour Krey Research Corporation are two national firms with branches in Chippewa Falls.

Enter Spectrum Corporation

Another force in the city's development has been the Spectrum Corporation, a general partnership of some 30 local investors who have financed and/or operated several educational materials, typesetting and plastics companies. The partners in Spectrum are not "captains of

Reprinted with permission from "Town Benefits When Citizens Keep Investment Dollars Home," *National Community Reporter,* published by the National Association of Towns and Townships, January 1984. Further information is available from NATaT, 1522 K Street, N.W., Suite 730, Washington, D.C., 20005, (202) 737-5200.

industry" looking for tax advantages, but local citizens wishing to invest in the economic growth of their town. In 1976, the partnership voted to diversify its holdings by purchasing the Hubbard Scientific Corporation of Northbrook, Illinois, manufacturer of educational products such as maps, globes, and planetariums and developer of educational curricula for disadvantaged and handicapped students.

After the purchase, a new plant, designed for 55 employees, was built in Chippewa Falls. The construction was financed through local banks with backing of the Spectrum Corporation. While Hubbard's research and design activities remain in Illinois, shareholders decided to move the manufacturing operations to Chippewa Falls to facilitate management and to bring much-needed jobs into the area.

By 1982 the new plant was so successful that Hubbard's director of operations, Dave Hancock, drew up expansion plans. Hancock wanted to increase plant capacity as the nation pulled out of its prolonged recession, but he projected the $800,000 expansion was not economically feasible if capital funds were borrowed at the conventional interest rate of 13 to 14 percent.

With Spectrum's assets already tied up in the purchase of the Hubbard Corporation, Hancock approached the city of Chippewa Falls for financing. Realizing that 30 new jobs depended on lower-than-conventional interest rates, the city agreed to issue industrial development bonds for the Hubbard expansion.

Bonds to finance industrial development

In simplest terms, an industrial development bond is a tax-exempt bond issued by a legally established unit of government for the financial benefit of a private business. In most cases, the public benefits from increased jobs or economic activity, the government benefits from increased tax revenues and the business benefits from borrowing money at a reduced interest rate because the bonds are tax exempt.

Once more the cooperation among Chippewa Falls' city government, private investors and lending institutions was the key to a local economic development project. Together these groups addressed the questions of who would issue the bonds, who would guarantee the bonds and who would buy the bonds.

The city of Chippewa Falls agreed to issue the bonds at 9 percent interest, approximately the same rate as tax-exempt municipal bonds. The principal and interest are to be repaid by the increased profits from the Hubbard Scientific Corporation. The city was not required to back the bonds with either its full faith and credit or any future city revenues.

The bonds have been guaranteed by seven local investors who are also part of the Spectrum Corporation. In addition to this personal guarantee, the bonds are backed by first and second mortgages on the plant expansion. While the investors will benefit directly from the future profits of the Hubbard Scientific Corporation, they may not purchase or benefit from the tax-exempt bond issue.

Two local banks purchased $600,000 worth of bonds, and two local, private investors each purchased $100,000 worth of bonds to complete the sale.

Local capital is key

The bonds have been sold, the plant has been built and 30 new employees are working at the Hubbard Scientific Corporation. Hancock says none of these things would have been possible without local capital for expansion at lower-than-conventional interest rates.

Communities of any size can learn from the example of Chippewa Falls. Citizens with funds to invest must be given the opportunity and incentive to make their investments locally. City and town officials must establish formal and informal contacts with local business and banking interests and encourage responsible development through informed zoning and taxing decisions.

Like Chippewa Falls, local governments that can legally do so may consider the use of industrial revenue bonds judicious. While these bonds have been criticized for benefiting large corporations and depleting federal tax revenues, the bonds have been essential in the economic development plans of many small and medium-sized governments. A strong case can be made that the new jobs and increased local taxes in communities like Chippewa Falls more than compensate for the loss of federal tax income.

For Further Reference

Part 1: Change: The Local Economy and the Local Government Role

Butler, Stuart M. *Enterprise Zones: Greenlining the Inner Cities*. New York: Universe Books, 1981.

Choate, Pat. "Manufacturing: Meeting the Global Competition." CUED *Commentary*, winter 1983, pp. 3-7.

Hirschman, Elizabeth C., and Rosenberg, Larry J. "Retailing without Stores." *Harvard Business Review*, July-August 1980, pp. 103-12.

Peterson, Peter G. "Curing the American Export Malady." *Business Week*, 16 August 1982, pp. 10-11.

Richman, Tom. "What America Needs Is a Few Good Failures." *Inc.*, September 1983, pp. 63-72.

Ummel, John. "Will Business Help Solve Local Housing Problems?" *Western City*, June 1983, pp. 6-8.

Part 2: Organizing for Economic Development

Conley, G., et al. *Economic Development: New Roles for City Government*. Washington, D.C.: U.S. Conference of Mayors, National Community Development Association, and Urban Land Institute, September 1979.

D'Alessio, Walter. "Economic Development As a Part of the Community Process: Philadelphia's I.D.C. Suggests How to Organize and Conduct an ED Program." *Journal of Housing*, March 1976, pp. 129-131.

Local Economic Development: A Strategic Approach. Training package. Washington, D.C.: International City Management Association, 1984.

National Council for Urban Economic Development. *An Introduction to the Economic Development Planning Process*. Washington, D.C.: CUED, July 1980.

Wolman, Harold. *Making Local Economic Development Decisions: A Framework for Local Officials*. Urban Institute Working Paper No. 1264-01. Washington, D.C.: The Urban Institute, January 1979.

Part 3: Public Sector Intervention in the Marketplace

Ady, Robert M. "High Technology Plants: Different Criteria for the Best Location." CUED *Commentary*, winter 1983, pp. 8-10.

Borut, Allan. "Promoting Real Estate Development." *Public Management*, September 1979, pp. 2-5.

Dickson, David G. "How Towns Can Attract Industry." *Virginia Town and City*, December 1981, pp. 4, 5, 7.

Ewing, Reid. "Some Principles of Business Loan Program Design." *Urban Land*, April 1981, pp. 8–13.

Herr, Philip B., et al. *Negotiating Fiscal Impacts: A Handbook for Evaluating City Development*. Boston, Mass.: Coalition of Northeast Municipalities, 1979.

Knight, Fred S. "Tax Increment Financing: A Tool for Redevelopment." Municipal Innovations Series, no. 6. Washington, D.C.: International City Management Association, February 1976.

McGuinness, Dan. "Convention Centers: Too Much of a Good Thing?" *Planning*, November 1982, pp. 13–17.

Mason, Patrick F., and Skinner, Donald J. "Raking in the Chips." *Planning*, November 1981, pp. 10–13.

Matzer, John, Jr., ed. *Capital Financing Strategies for Local Governments*, part 4, "Economic Development and Redevelopment Financing Techniques." Washington, D.C.: International City Management Association, 1983.

Morse, George, and Rohrer, John. "Do Local Development Incentives Pay Off?" *Ohio Cities and Villages*, August 1982, pp. 30–34.

Rosen, Corey, and Whyte, William F. "Employee Ownership: Saving Businesses, Saving Jobs." CUED *Commentary*, spring 1982, pp. 16–19.

Urban Land Institute. *Adaptive Use: Development Economics, Process, and Profiles*. Washington, D.C.: Urban Land Institute, 1978.

Part 4: Successful Local Programs

Barbour, George P., Jr., and King, James R. "Business Retention: Holding on to What You've Already Got." *Public Management*, September 1979, pp. 11–13.

Brandon, Dennis. "Suburban Renewal: Public Sponsored Industrial Development." *Urban Land*, June 1982, pp. 15–19.

Burris, Lance. "Richmond, California: A Case Study in Economic Development." *Urban Land*, May 1980, pp. 9–17.

Cisneros, Henry G. "San Antonio's Place in the Technology Economy: A Review of Opportunities and a Blueprint for Action." City of San Antonio, September 1982.

Pizzano, Arthur E. "How to Keep Local Businesses from Straying." *Planning*, May 1982, pp. 13–15.

Stark, Nancy T. "Industrial Plant Closings: A Community Responds." Municipal Innovations Series, no. 36. Washington, D.C.: International City Management Association, summer 1982.

Practical Management Series

**Shaping the Local Economy:
Current Perspectives on Economic Development**

Text type
Century Expanded

Composition
Unicorn Graphics
Washington, D.C.

Printing and binding
R. R. Donnelley & Sons Company
Harrisonburg, Virginia

Cover design
Rebecca Geanaros